The Essence of
JESUS

The Essence of
JESUS

ARTHUR ROWE

CHARTWELL
BOOKS, INC.

This edition printed in 2006 by
CHARTWELL BOOKS, INC.
A Division of **BOOK SALES, INC.**
114 Northfield Avenue
Edison, New Jersey 08837

ISBN-13: 978-0-7858-2115-1
ISBN-10: 0-7858-2115-5

Printed in China

Cover illustration: The Cloister of St Catherine Church,
Bethlehem

Contents

Preface   1

Introduction   3

Chapter 1: Jesus, the evidence   7

Chapter 2: Jesus in the Gospels   27

Chapter 3: Jesus and the first Christians   51

Chapter 4: Jesus and the emergence of Christianity   75

Chapter 5: Jesus in an age of devotion   101

Chapter 6: Jesus in word and sacrament   123

Chapter 7: Jesus of history and Christ of faith   151

Chapter 8: Jesus and other religions   177

Chapter 9: Jesus today   199

Glossary   218

Bibliography   221

Index   225

To the memory of my parents, who taught me
the most important things I know

Preface

My heartfelt thanks go to those who read drafts of chapters or the whole book and offered me invaluable advice, encouragement and correction. They include my patient wife, Pam, always my first critic, who has saved my blushes with others. The others included: Roy Boyer, David Golder, Pieter Lalleman, Judy Powles, Ian Randall, Debra Reid, Paul Scott-Evans, Alison and David Southall, and Stephen Wright, colleagues at Spurgeon's College, London, and friends. My thanks also to Dr Penelope Hall for permitting me to include matters from our talk during her visit to Spurgeon's College.

Three technical matters. First, in dating people's lives and events I have followed the fashionable convention of replacing BC and AD with BCE, standing for Before the Common Era, and CE for the Common Era. But as F. F. Bruce pointed out some years ago, 'the fact remains that the reckoning of the years runs forward and backward from the date of Jesus' birth, as calculated (not as accurately as might have been wished) by Dionysius Exiguus in the sixth century' (*The Real Jesus*, London: Hodder & Stoughton, 1985, p. 209). Secondly, I am very indebted to the books and resources listed in the bibliography. References to writers or quotations in the main text are to these sources. Thirdly, references to the Bible in the form 1 Corinthians 15:3 mean Paul's First Letter to the Corinthians Chapter 15, verse 3.

Introduction

What is meant by 'the essence of Jesus'? What is meant by 'the essence' of anything? Cassell's *New English Dictionary* includes in its definition of the word 'that which constitutes the nature of something, that which makes it what it is'. In the case of most world faiths, the essence of that faith lies in its teachings. So, for example, when the Buddha was dying or 'passing into *Nirvana*' (as Buddhists put it), he pointed his disciples to his teachings, not to himself. This makes the attempt to understand that faith in some ways more straightforward than the attempt to understand the essence of Jesus. You can only really come to understand a person by getting to know that individual. Certainly the essence of Jesus involves more than just his teaching. It is quintessentially connected with who he is as well. And notice that this statement is written in the present tense – *who he is* – because it is essential to the Christian faith that Jesus be not just a hazy figure from the past but continues to be present wherever his disciples congregate (Gospel of Matthew, 18:20), and in the lives of individuals who invite him in (Revelations, 3:20).

But how can we approach the essence of Jesus? The aim of this book is to try and visualize the figure of Jesus as people have seen him between the 1st and 21st centuries. He undeniably left powerful impressions on the lives of important men and women down the centuries, an influence reflected in works of literature, art, music, drama, worship and scholarship. My intention is to provoke a sympathetic but not uncritical appreciation of the many different expressions of faith in Jesus. We will walk in the footsteps of different kinds of believers, including followers of other faiths as well as our contemporaries. One of the underlying assumptions in this book is that sceptics, too, are believers. The content of their beliefs may differ from those of people committed to one of the major faiths, but no human being can possibly think about anyone or anything without some kind of framework for their faith. At the same time, it is an open challenge to everyone to test these ideas about Jesus and their various expressions by comparing them with portraits in the New Testament, available to people in every continent today.

Why should the New Testament be given this defining role? Its writings, which all stem from the 1st century CE, are our earliest sources. These include the Gospels of the four Evangelists which are remarkable documents. Although written after that most extraordinary of historical events, the Resurrection of Jesus, they reliably reflect the memories of Jesus' closest friends. For example, they show how little these people really understood Jesus and what he was trying to say during his ministry. After the Resurrection and the gift of God's Spirit, they came to understand more, as the Book of Acts illustrates. But they did not then revise their earlier misunderstandings when they recounted the story of their first three years in the presence of Jesus, they let these inaccuracies stand. Neither did they revise those issues which arose in the early churches during the ministry of Jesus, or propose possible solutions which he might have offered to later problems. For example, the question of whether gentile Christians should be circumcised led to the formation of the Council of Jerusalem and was an issue which Paul addressed in his correspondence with the churches of Galatia. Had Jesus spoken about this, they could have appealed to his words. But no such words ever existed and the Gospels do not anticipate this problem. The letters which follow the Book of Acts in the New Testament explain the Christian faith and how it is to be lived out in practice. The New Testament constitutes the defining elements for a Christian understanding of the essence of Jesus.

Following the first chapter of this book, which examines the evidence for Jesus and the reliability of the New Testament documents, the next two chapters summarize these defining elements. They show us the earliest accounts of who he was, what he did and what he taught. From Chapter 4 onwards, we sample great slices of history: from the beginning of the 2nd to the end of the 5th century, from the 6th century to the invention of printing in the 15th century, the Reformation and its aftermath (16th–17th century), the Enlightenment to the end of the millennium (18th–20th century). One chapter is reserved for the views of writers from other faiths and the last chapter deals largely with the new century. Inevitably the boundaries of these historical periods are not set in stone, and they sometimes overlap. A lack of adherence to strict chronology within particular chapters may offend some historians. But my objective is to open up pictures of different kinds and to introduce readers to encounters with people and their direct experiences of Jesus which might help to create new possibilities for coming to see him with greater clarity.

Chapter 1

Jesus, the evidence

Jesus is the most famous man in history and has more followers in the world today than at any time since he lived in Palestine over 2,000 years ago. His reputation is that of a good man, a teacher and a healer who went about doing good works. Yet he was arrested, tried and executed as a terrorist by the Roman authorities. Execution by crucifixion was one of the most brutal ways of killing ever recorded, and it was used to put to death enemies of the state. It was a warning devised by the Roman authorities to deter potential rebels. So why did Jesus, who was such a good man, die in this manner? And how did it come about that this apparently ignominious demise was not the end of the story but the beginning of all as far as Jesus of Nazareth was concerned?

HOW DO WE KNOW ABOUT JESUS?

What do we really know about Jesus and how can we know more? How do we know anything about any historical figure for that matter? We can study the evidence that survives from that time and relate this to other information that we have of the place and time in which he is said to have lived and gradually we are able to construct a picture of what he was possibly or probably like. Hence what evidence do we have for Jesus? Our principal sources are the four Gospels and other writings that make up the New Testament. We will consider the nature of these in a moment but first it is interesting to consider some of the references to Jesus outside of the New Testament. There are references in both Jewish and Roman writings which survive as evidence for the life of Jesus and some surprising aspects of his life.

Jewish references

The Jewish historian Josephus [37–100 CE] makes two references to Jesus in his history of the Jewish people which was published in 93–94 CE. In the longer reference, he wrote something like:

> At this time there appeared Jesus, a wise man. For he was a doer of startling deeds, a teacher of people who received the truth with pleasure. And he gained a following both among many Jews and among many of Greek origin. And when [Pontius] Pilate, because of an accusation made by the leading men among us, condemned him to the Cross, those who previously loved him did not cease to do so. And, up until this very day, the tribe of Christians (named after him) has not died out.
>
> *(Jewish Antiquities* 18.63–64)

I say 'something like' because many scholars think that the text was edited by Christians but this version of what Josephus probably wrote, which has filtered out possible Christian phrases, is widely accepted (Dunn, p. 141). The second reference to Jesus refers back to this passage and is an account of his execution by James, who is described as 'the brother of Jesus who is called the Messiah' (*Jewish Antiquities*, 20.200). Josephus tells us that Jesus did indeed exist and was both a respected teacher and someone who performed miraculous deeds; that he was accused by the Jewish leaders and Pontius Pilate ordered his execution; that his death did not mark the end of his movement for followers continued to be active at the time when Josephus was writing.

In Jewish rabbi writings, which are difficult to date, there is a reference to *Yeshua* (Jesus), who is described as a magician who led Israel astray and it says that he was hanged on the eve of Passover (*Babylonian Talmud Sanhedrin* 43a). Here again is a possible allusion to Jesus' miracles; to his teachings which were not supported by the Jewish authorities of the time; and to his execution at Passover.

Roman references

The Roman historian Tacitus [55–120 CE], writing early in the 2nd century about the fire that swept through Rome during the reign of Nero [64 CE], declares that blame was placed on certain 'Christians. Their name comes from Christ who, during Tiberius' reign, had been executed by the procurator Pontius Pilate' (*Annals* 15.44). Since 'Christ' was another name for Jesus this is a clear reference to his Crucifixion. Suetonius [70–130 CE], another Roman historian writing about an incident during the time of Emperor Claudius [c. 49 CE], says that 'since the Jews were constantly causing disturbances at the instigation of Chrestus, he [Claudius] expelled them from Rome' (*Claudius* 25.4). This coincides with a note in Acts 18:2 about Aquila and his wife, Priscilla, both of whom were Jews, having recently come to Corinth from Rome 'because Claudius had commanded all Jews to leave Rome'. But the reference to 'Chrestus' is believed to be in actuality referring to 'Christus' (Christ) and the disturbances may have been caused by someone preaching that Jesus was the Messiah.

These references from writers outside of the New Testament do not add anything to what the New Testament already tells us and it might even be said that they constitute rather thin testimony. They do indicate, however, that Jesus was an historical figure well-known for performing remarkable deeds, who had gained followers and was indeed crucified under Pilate's jurisdiction. They also indicate that, following Jesus' death, Christians had not ceased to exist. There were disturbances among the Jews over this man and some people were declaring that he was the Messiah.

The first reference to Christians in official correspondence appears in a letter sent by Pliny the Younger [61–113 CE], then governor of Bithynia, to Emperor Trajan in 112 CE. The governor asks his regent for advice on how to deal with the Christians. He says that they claimed 'their fault or error had been this, that it was their habit on a fixed day to assemble before daylight and recite in turns a form of words to Christ as a god; and they bound themselves with an oath, not for any crime, but not to commit theft or robbery or adultery, not to break their word' and so on. Pliny adds that the spread of 'this superstition' was threatening the livelihood of those farmers who supplied animals for sacrifice in temples. It is clear that these Christians who worshipped Christ were regarded as subversive, a threat to the state and the economy. The governor thought they should be executed if they did not renounce their faith. When evidence like this is combined with early 2nd century references to churches in Palestine, Asia Minor, Greece, Italy, some of the Mediterranean islands, Egypt and North Africa, we obtain a clearer picture of the vigorous growth of the Christian Church despite persecution and the original execution of Jesus.

The New Testament

For more information about Jesus' life, we turn to the New Testament. The earliest documents are the letters of Paul and he quotes beliefs about Jesus which he himself had been taught, probably as early as two years after the Crucifixion. For example, in his First Letter to the Corinthians, Paul tells us not only that Christ died but begins to explain why he died. For accounts of the life and work of Jesus, however, we should turn to the four Gospels, all of which were written during the 1st century.

Who were the apostles Matthew, Mark, Luke and John? Matthew and John were two of Jesus' closest disciples, men who had left their homes and abandoned their livelihoods to follow this new teacher. Matthew was called from the tax office and John and his brother, James, had been fishermen. They were among the twelve whom Jesus called the 'apostles', individuals he trained to go and deliver his work and spread his message. Mark was apparently a young man who made a fleeting and unnamed appearance in his Gospel. His mother's home was a meeting place for the early church in Jerusalem, where Peter turned for refuge when he escaped from prison. Mark accompanied Paul and Barnabas for part of their first missionary journey. Luke was also one of Paul's friends and accompanied him on several of his important journeys. In his letter to the Colossians, Paul refers to him as 'my dear friend, the doctor'.

HOW SHOULD WE TREAT THESE SOURCES?

A common view held from the 18th century well into the 20th century about an historian was that he simply sat down before historical evidence, examined it and then wrote down an objective and impartial account of what had happened based on the facts before him. It has been increasingly realized since then that no human being can ever produce a purely objective account uncontaminated by that person's values and beliefs. While there are some objective facts which are true for most people, the bigger questions, such as those raised about Jesus, require judgment, and judgment is coloured by one's view of the world, one's beliefs and values.

Consider two examples. It might be argued that one of the most objective things about Jesus Christ was the fact he was crucified. As we have seen, this is attested in both Jewish and Roman sources, as well as the New Testament. But the majority of Muslims refuse to accept this on the basis of a reference in the *Qur'an* (*Surah* 4.157) which denies Jesus was ever crucified. Since for Muslims the *Qur'an* is divine revelation, no amount of historical evidence or research can contradict or qualify it for them. In addition, they are unable to accept that God (*Allah*) would have allowed one of his prophets (Jesus, that is) to die a cursed death. Muslims deduce that crucifixion was a dishonourable death from Deuteronomy 21:23. They accept this verse as having divine revelatory status because both Jews and Christians had in the past received authentic revelations from *Allah*. When a prophet is ignored, insulted or threatened in the *Qur'an*, *Allah* punishes the village or town responsible and defends his servant. So, according to their world view, it is illogical to suppose Jesus was crucified. Consider the 19th century German theologian David Strauss

[1808–74] as a second example. In his *Life of Jesus*, Strauss denies that the supernatural elements in the Gospels were historical events because he holds a view of the universe as a closed system of cause-and-effect from which miracles or divine interventions are totally excluded. He calls these accounts 'myths', or stories written to demonstrate the compassion of Jesus in action.

Both of these examples show that people's world views do indeed influence their assessment of historical evidence irrespective of whether this stems from Christian or non-Christian sources. This is true of historians writing today, which is why we get different accounts of the lives of historically significant people. This is also true of writers of documents from the past which have survived. Therefore it is fair to say that there is no neutral, impartial place for anyone, past or present, to stand, nor is there enough objective evidence available to write a completely impartial history. Any attempt to do so would leave out the most interesting parts. Consequently we have to recognize that Jesus, like any other historical figure, is inevitably interpreted and understood by different people in different ways; everyone approaches him, and the evidence about him, from their own particular world view. Even concrete evidence has to be interpreted within a framework.

This does not mean that it is impossible to agree on anything, or that some might present a more believable portrait of Jesus than others. Even the judgment that one portrait is more believable than another is largely influenced by the values and beliefs which a reader brings to a reading. It is natural for communities with similar beliefs to also share a similar understanding. It does not follow from this that the study of history is a waste of time. Some facts can be established on the basis of evidence and good judgement. The claim that what writers produce is coloured by their view of the world does not tell us anything about the value of the information that is provided. It simply prepares us for the fact that we must take their personal views into account. We can adjust our understanding of events by reading different accounts and considering as much of the available evidence as possible. When we read the Gospels, we must do so with an awareness that each writer has his own perspective and purpose, yet recognize that this does not make the events described necessarily fiction. This also means that some interpretations account for the evidence better than others. The better interpretations will account for the bigger picture and include more of the available evidence. It is not unusual for people to approach the Gospels with their minds made up beforehand. They are therefore not surprised to find their ideas confirmed and will not learn anything new. Those who come with more of an open mind will often be surprised. They may experience something like what J. B. Phillips had to deal with when he was translating the New Testament. He wrote that it was like 'rewiring a house with the current still switched on'.

To know an historical figure is to interpret him in a particular context so we have different Christian, Jewish, Muslim and even Hindu views of Jesus, not to mention the opinions of those with a sceptical frame of mind. But it is up to each one of us to test these various views by reading the evidence and evaluating the pictures we are given in terms of that evidence for ourselves. It is helpful to treat sources, such as testimonies or witnesses, as evidence from those who came to know and believe Jesus to be the kind of person they present, or in the case of the Roman authorities, the cause of a movement that for one reason or another was a nuisance.

HOW GOOD IS OUR DOCUMENTARY EVIDENCE FOR JESUS?

It has long been thought that the nearer historical evidence is to the time and people with which it deals, the more reliable or useful it is. This judgment needs to be exercised with caution, but on this basis, we can compare hard manuscript evidence from New Testament writings, our best sources for Jesus, with documentary evidence for other historical figures and their writings.

Manuscript evidence for some classical works

Julius Caesar's *Gallic War* was written between 58 and 50 BCE, but only nine or ten manuscripts are still in use today and the oldest of these dates to 900 years after the events. Livy's history of Rome was written between 59 BC and 17 CE. In this case, scholars depend on twenty manuscripts. Only one of these, containing fragments of Books III–IV, is as old as the fourth century CE.

In the case of Tacitus and the Greek historians Thucydides [460–400 BCE] and Herodotus [480–425 BCE], the copies of their works available today date from the 9th century CE or even later. Despite the gap of centuries between the original writings and these copies, most historians are happy to draw on them for evidence. Without them, historians would be able to say very little at all.

Manuscript evidence for New Testament writings

When we turn to documentary evidence for the New Testament, it is a different story, and the evidence for securing a version of the text which is as close as possible to what was originally written is abundant. Not only that, but witnesses can be traced back to within two or three generations of the events themselves. If the Crucifixion of Jesus took place about the year 30 and the Gospels were written on the majority view as follows – Matthew 85–90, Mark about 65, Luke 80–85, and John 90–100 – then there were people still alive when these were written who could remember what Jesus had said and done. Evidently these people were reaching the end of their lives and one reason the Gospels were written down may well have been to preserve the oral traditions handed down by eyewitnesses, as Luke himself hints at (1:1–2).

Given that none of the original New Testament writings still exist, there are well over 5,000 manuscripts, all of which are copies of copies going back to the original source. The earliest is a fragment of John's Gospel, usually dated about 125 CE. It has John 18:31–33 on one side and verses 37–38 on the other. Found in Egypt, it is now kept in the John Rylands Library in Manchester. John's Gospel is thought to have been written in Ephesus, Turkey, between 90 and 100 CE, and yet within a generation, a copy came to Egypt from which this tiny manuscript survives. This indicates that an early Christian document travelled through the Roman world and was read by Christians in different parts of the empire. The short letters in the New Testament may have been written on single sheets of papyrus (see 2 John 12) but the larger books, like the Gospels, would have been written on scrolls. It was not long before it was found much more convenient to put collections of writings together in a book, a *codex* [plural: *codices*]. In fact, the Rylands fragment came from a *codex* and not a roll. The use of both sides of the papyrus sheets is evidence for that.

For anything like full texts of the Gospels we need to look at a century or so later. The *Codex Sinaiticus*, a 4th century book which contains part of the Old Testament and all of the New Testament plus some additional books, is on display at the British

Library. Discovered by the text critic Constantine von Tischendorf halfway through the 19th century at St Catherine's monastery on Mount Sinai, the British government bought it from the Russians for £100,000 on Christmas Day in 1933. Other 4th and 5th century *codices* are the *Vaticanus* and *Alexandrinus*, each of which contains nearly all of the Bible, including virtually all the Gospels. In addition there are thousands of larger or smaller fragmentary manuscripts, many dating from the 2nd and 3rd centuries. Teams of scholars dedicate their lives to studying, classifying and comparing these pieces of a huge jigsaw. When this evidence is compared with early translations into other languages and quotations from the writings of the early Church Fathers, we begin to get an impression of the weight of evidence for a reliable reconstruction of the actual text of the writings of the New Testament. Published editions of the New Testament now give us a standardized version of the text, and although painstaking study of the evidence continues, scholars now confidently rely on it for most purposes.

Other manuscripts, other gospels

In 1945 some peasants found a large jar containing eleven *codices* and fragments of two others in a cave about 80 kilometres downstream from Luxor on the Nile in Egypt. The 52 texts [twelve of which are duplicates] are now known as the Nag Hammadi Library, named after the nearest modern town in the area. They are written in Coptic, a form of the ancient language of Egypt. They contain a number of gospels which are different from those in the New Testament. Fragments in Greek of some of these had been known to exist. The most famous is the *Gospel of Thomas*, a collection of 114 sayings by Jesus. The texts of other gospels include the *Gospel of Philip*, the *Gospel of the Egyptians* and the *Gospel of Truth*. There are also various quotations by Jesus scattered in some of the other texts. But not all of the texts are by any means biblical. For example, we will consider an extract from Plato's *Republic* and the contents of these gospels at a later point. What we need to note here is the date of these documents. They must have been written before they were hidden towards the end of the 4th century but they were most probably penned a century after the New Testament Gospels. Despite claims in the media from time to time, and some from eccentric scholars, they are evidence for what people wrote and believed during the early centuries of the Christian Church rather than alternative, reliable sources for the historical Jesus.

WHY ARE THERE FOUR GOSPELS IN THE NEW TESTAMENT?

Connections with the Apostles

Strictly speaking, the four Gospels are anonymous documents. The names Matthew, Mark, Luke and John may have been added later once the scrolls were collected as an early church librarian might have wanted to be able to distinguish them from each other and other scrolls. Whoever was responsible for this would have believed the names Matthew, Mark, Luke and John to have had some connection to the scrolls. Papias [*c.* 60–130 CE], Bishop of Hierapolis in Asia Minor, is quoted by the early Church historian Eusebius [260–340 CE] as saying: 'The elder used to say, "Mark, who had been Peter's interpreter, wrote down carefully, but not in order, all that he remembered of the Lord's sayings and doings. For he had not heard the Lord or been one of his followers, but later, as I said, one of Peter's."' It is not clear who the elder was but Papias had it on good authority that Mark's Gospel was a version of Peter preaching. We hear from the same source that Matthew 'collected the sayings of the Lord in Aramaic and everyone translated these as best as they could'.

Irenaeus [*c.* 130–200 CE], Bishop of Lyons, attributed both the Gospel of Luke and the Book of Acts to Luke, Paul's fellow traveller. The same writer attributes the fourth gospel to John, who wrote it in Ephesus (*Against All Heresies*, 3.1.1). Although some scholars approach these testimonies with scepticism, which leads them to suppose that any alternative explanation contrived is better than the slender evidence available, not a great deal is to be gained by following those alternatives. Halfway through the 2nd century, Justin Martyr [100–165 CE] speaks of the public reading of the 'memoirs of the Apostles' alongside the Old Testament as scripture in church and, by the end of the century, Irenaeus is writing about the four-fold gospel.

As early as the 2nd century there is evidence that four Gospels carrying apostolic authority were in fact in circulation. We have seen how Mark's authority was derived from Peter and Luke's leadership was the direct result of his association with Paul. None of the four Gospels can therefore be regarded in isolation. In the middle of the 2nd century, Marcion [80–155 CE], a wealthy ship owner from Sinope in Pontus (modern-day Turkey), made his way to Rome where he joined a church. Convinced that the Christian faith should sever all ties with Judaism and the Old Testament, he was the first to produce a list of books of Holy Scripture. His Bible consisted of the Gospel of Luke, with all the Jewish bits deleted, and ten letters by his hero, the Apostle Paul. This stimulated others within the Church to respond. The African Church Father Tertullian [160–220 CE] wrote a five-volume work against Marcion [*c.* 207 CE], and by this time, Irenaeus was writing that it was as natural for the Church to have four pillars (the Gospels) as there were four winds from Heaven and the four corners of the world. Towards the end of the 2nd century, a list of books now known as the Muratorian canon (after L. A. Muratori who discovered it in 1740), notes that Luke is the third gospel and John the fourth. The beginning of the document is damaged but it is reasonable to assume that Matthew and Mark were the first and second gospels mentioned in the list.

The canon

The word 'canon' translates as 'measuring rod' or 'rule' and came to be used in the context of authoritative lists of books by which one could measure one's faith. Before there were such lists of books, there were creeds or statements of faith which were used as tests. These were not just used as weapons against other faiths but as means of teaching new Christians and those seeking self-assurance. The use of the word 'canon' for a list of biblical books is found for the first time in the Easter letter of Athanasius, Bishop of Alexandria [367 CE], which includes a list that corresponds almost exactly with the Old and New Testaments. Athanasius was concerned by the appearance of heretical or spurious books which had been introduced by dissident factions and he wrote to help his church by indicating those books within the canon which were divinely inspired.

HOW ARE THE FOUR GOSPELS TO BE USED?

The differences between the four Gospels plus any striking similarities, particularly between the first three gospels, all of which have a common or 'synoptic' view of Jesus in common, pose problems. These three gospels are sometimes set out in parallel columns in a synopsis so that any similarities and differences can be clearly seen. This is is known as 'the synoptic problem'. Various solutions have been proposed, including that all four Gospels draw on a common oral tradition from which they draw selectively, or that one gospel was adapted by the other three Evangelists in different ways.

An attempt was made within the early church to replace the four Gospels with one in which the evidence presented in the other three could be woven into one reliable account [Tatian's *Diatessaron*, *c*. 150]. This version was rejected by Irenaeus in his work against heresies. For seventeen centuries, Matthew was regarded as the first written Gospel as it supplied the framework, shape and colour for the image of Jesus Christ presented by the Church. By the end of the 19th century, however, Mark came to replace Matthew in terms of popularity, and has remained the favourite gospel ever since. In the 20th century, most gospel studies fragmented the four Gospels, which were treated as mosaics broken up with a view to one day providing a fuller picture. Things changed in the second half of the century and attention shifted to treating each gospel as a whole. It is now generally recognized we have four distinct portraits of Jesus, all of which are complementary accounts. To understand the story they tell from a responsible and historical point of view, we need to have some acquaintance with the historical context to which these events relate.

THE CONTEXT OF THE 1ST-CENTURY WORLD

A Roman world

Jesus was born into a world dominated by the Roman Empire. Emperor Octavian [63 BCE–14 CE] founded the empire in 27 BCE after a grateful senate rewarded him for ending civil war and establishing peace in which trade and prosperity could flourish. They gave him the right to command all Roman legions and honoured him with the title of 'Augustus', meaning 'one to be revered'. The empire was divided into provinces administered by governors and client kings. The latter were either existing kings who agreed to serve the emperor or people appointed by Rome. Jesus lived his short life in the province of Syria, an imperial province on the eastern borders of the empire, where Roman legions were stationed to defend the borders. Within the province were various client kings – Herod the Great until 4 BCE and then his kingdom was divided between his sons Archelaus, Herod Antipas and Herod Philip. Jesus' public ministry was conducted in Galilee, the territory of Herod Antipas, and in Judea, under Pontius Pilate, one of the Roman governors who had replaced Archelaus in 26 CE. It is not surprising to find Jesus meeting a Roman centurion or tax collectors (Jews who were working for the occupying power) and rebels who wanted to fight for Jewish freedom.

A Jewish world

Jesus was a Jew and he lived and worked among Jews, so it is important to know something about Judaism in the 1st century. The epicentre of the Jewish world at the time was Jerusalem, the city known in their Holy Scriptures as the city of God. Until 70 CE, there was a temple here. Herod the Great had begun an extensive rebuilding programme in 19 BCE which was not completed until 64 CE. This was the temple which the disciples pointed out to Jesus (Mark 13:1), where daily sacrifices were carried out by priests, and the focal point for the three annual festivals of Passover, Pentecost and Tabernacles, during which Jews congregated in the city in vast numbers. The spiritual heart of Judaism was the *Torah*, (the Law), and in the Law, the one-ness of God and the command to love God wholeheartedly as set out in the *Shema* (the word means 'hear' and is the first word of Deuteronomy 6:4–5). Whatever their differences, Jews were united in their belief that the one God had committed himself to their ancestors, and therefore to them, through a covenant at Mount Sinai in the time of Moses. There was also an oral law which taught how the written law was to be applied to the details of daily life. This oral law is called 'the traditions of the elders' in the Gospels. It was neither simple nor agreed and Jews were divided into different groups according to their response to the oral law. They also differed in their attitudes to Roman occupation. Many longed for God to act and fulfil his promises through the prophets to send a great king like David, a Messiah, to deliver the people and put a restored Israel at the centre of the world. Others were nervous about anything that might disturb the status quo in which they had vested interests. We meet most of these groups in the Gospels.

The vast majority [90 per cent] were the 'people of the land' who resented taxation and being conscripted for service but they welcomed the peace and security which the Romans brought. Perhaps they dreamed of independence. The Pharisees were a small party, only about 6,000 out of a population of 1–2 million. Most of them lived in Judea, in or near Jerusalem. They tried to observe and teach the Law in all its details. They had a saying that if all the people kept to the Law for one day the Messiah would come. They looked for God's intervention to deliver them from Rome. The Sadducees were an even smaller group than the Pharisees. Members of wealthy, aristocratic families from Jerusalem, many of them were priests. Their policy was co-operation with the Romans in order to keep the status quo and practise the temple cult which they believed essential to maintaining a good relationship between God and his people. The Essenes are not mentioned in the New Testament but are known from Josephus the Jewish historian and Philo the biblical scholar. They had even stricter rules than the Pharisees and generally lived in communities with carefully controlled contacts with the outside world. Most scholars identify the community at Qumran, down by the Dead Sea, with the Essenes. They had withdrawn, not in protest against the Romans but against Jewish leaders who, they thought, had sold out to contemporary fashions and culture. Finally there were revolutionary terrorists or freedom fighters (sometimes referred to as 'zealots') with whom Jesus is occasionally identified. They were responsible for several outbreaks of revolution culminating in the war of 66–73 CE.

Jesus was frequently found in the synagogues, the local centres for Jewish meetings, worship and education. The ruler of the synagogue was usually a prominent, wealthy member of the congregation who took on the responsibility for the upkeep of the building and had some role in the ordering of the events that took place there. There were synagogues all over Palestine and in most of the cities within the Roman Empire.

Other religions

The culture of the Roman world was one impregnated with Greek ideas, language, philosophy and religion. There was a growing scepticism about the ability of traditional gods to save human beings and society. There was an increasing cynicism and a darkness of spirit. Some people looked to the mystery religions for salvation. Others were resigned to make the best of life as it came, well aware of their limitations in the face of Fate. The 'mysteries' were secret societies, whose foundation myths were derived from the natural cycle of the year, and which offered followers deliverance from disaster, futility and death. There were different versions, such as the cult of Isis based on an Egyptian story of the god Osiris, a dying and rising god linked to the rise and fall of the Nile, or the Greek god Dionysus of Asia Minor who was associated with the fermentation of wine and the fertility of the earth. Participation in sacred meals united the worshipper with the god in death and life.

This then was the world into which Jesus was born when Emperor Augustus sent out an edict requesting a general registration for taxation purposes, a decree which forced Joseph and Mary to leave Nazareth and make their way to Bethlehem because he was of the Davidic line. This was the world in which Jesus began his public ministry as Luke puts it: 'in the fifteenth year of the reign of Tiberius Caesar, Pontius Pilate being governor of Judea and Herod being tetrarch of the region of Ituraea and Trachonitis, and Lysanias tetrarch of Abilene, during the high priesthood of Annas and Caiaphas'. In many ways, this is a foreign world and we must approach the people and the events that we come across through their eyes and with their world view in mind.

21ST CENTURY PERSPECTIVES

It is also important to be aware of the world views that we inevitably bring to our readings. In this first decade of the 21st century, there are still many people who think like the theologian David Strauss, people for whom the world is a closed system of cause-and-effect and for whom all explanations have to be given in terms of that system. They translate any language about God and his dealings with people into the languages of psychology, anthropology and even astronomy. So, for example, the late Francis Crick [1916–2004], one of the three scientists awarded the Nobel prize for discovering the structure of DNA, could only account for the origin of life on earth by reference to extraterrestrial invasion. But, during the last years of the 20th century, a renewed interest in spirituality has encouraged people to attend to the signals of a reality that goes beyond our empirical senses. There is also an increasing realization that, globally, more people live by faith within something bigger than themselves and their everyday concerns. This may help us prepare to suspend our scepticism and allow people from other ages to tell us how they saw Jesus.

Chapter 2

Jesus in the Gospels

It is time to pursue our quest for an answer to the question with which we began our discussion. Why *was* Jesus crucified? We will take two lines of approach to this question. First, we will make our way through the general story of the Gospels in order to understand the principal narrative. Second, we will consider the particular angle taken by each of the Gospels regarding this story. It is important to recall that these accounts are definitive for a Christian understanding of Jesus, and in that sense, later attempts to portray Jesus are judged in relation to these accounts.

THE STORY

John the Baptist

All four Gospels and the Book of Acts agree that the public ministry of Jesus was introduced by John the Baptist, who is introduced as something of a wild man wearing the clothes of a prophet, eating locusts and wild honey, and addressing crowds of people in the wilderness of Judea. The term 'wilderness' does not mean 'desert', but an 'abandoned or uncultivated place', and was of great significance to the history of the Jewish people. They had never forgotten the forty-year journey made by their ancestors through the wilderness from Egypt to the Promised Land. It was in the wilderness at Mount Sinai that they received the *Torah* (the Law) and were elected the people of God. The prophets had spoken of a return to the 'wilderness' and of a second exodus that would introduce the messianic age. It is therefore not surprising that several self-proclaimed messianic pretenders would gather their followers in such places. But John was no messianic pretender. He explicitly denied any such ambitions, describing himself as 'a voice of one crying in the wilderness', in the way of the Old Testament prophet Isaiah before him. The 2nd century Jewish document 1 Maccabees indicates that the days of the prophets were over (9:27). This had not, however, extinguished hope in God's prophets for here was a man dressed like the prophet Elijah of old (2 Kings 1:8) calling on the people to return to God who was about to act in sovereign power to set his people free. No wonder crowds from throughout Judea and beyond the Jordan flocked to hear John the Baptist, who baptized the faithful in the river by submerging them in water. Although the Jews may have remembered the crossing of the river Jordan years before by the Israelites as they entered the Promised Land, this act was seen primarily as a public confession of human sin and a preparation for God to act. A revolutionary movement with a difference was being set in motion.

The baptism of Jesus

John the Baptist prefigures this event and announces the arrival of someone greater than himself, saying he will not be worthy to be this man's slave. He further announces that this man will exercise the sovereign power of God in blessing and judgment. When Jesus arrives among the crowd, he asks to be baptized by John. The spectacle which John then witnesses following Jesus' baptism confirms to him that this indeed is the man he had spoken about. Here we come across one of those events which are difficult for us to picture with any sense of realism. In each of the Gospels, it says that, following the baptism, as Jesus came up out of the water, 'he saw the heavens open and the [Holy] Spirit descend like a dove'. A voice from Heaven (that of God) addresses him as the Son of God's love and pleasure. This is possibly a private experience which Jesus later relates to his disciples. The terms he uses gain significance from their Old Testament references. The parting of the heavens suggests an act of God is at work (Isaiah 64:1, Malachi 3:10) while the arrival of the Holy Spirit recalls the words of Isaiah which were read out by Jesus in the synagogue:

> The Spirit of the Lord is upon me, because he has anointed me to proclaim good news to the poor. He has sent me to proclaim liberty to the captives and recovering of sight to the blind, to set at liberty those who are oppressed, to proclaim the year of the Lord's favour.
>
> (Isaiah 61:1–2, Luke 4:16–20)

The words of the heavenly voice echo a much earlier address spoken by Isaiah (Psalm 2:7, Isaiah 42:1) about the king of Israel and the servant of the Lord. It is reasonable to suppose that, in this experience, Jesus *is* both Israel's king and the Son of God, now invested with the power to undertake the arduous task assigned to him.

The temptations

This event was followed by another remarkable experience which was once again presumably private to Jesus. It is what we call his temptations, although it would be a mistake to assume he did not experience acute temptation at other times. Once again he is in the wilderness, this time for a period of forty days. It has often been suggested that the number forty here echoes the number of years spent by the Israelites wandering the wilderness following their escape from Egypt. Hence Jesus may be reliving the story of his people. But evidently the subject of these temptations questions the very nature of the manner in which he is to undertake his mission. Most people have had some experience of temptation or test of character, where they have had to make decisions between possible courses of action, yet these tests are seldom attributed to the Devil. This is a way of reinstating a biblical theme that was first introduced in the story of Adam and Eve in the Book of Genesis. The invitation to turn stones into bread and jump down from the temple and be rescued by angels are both introduced with the words 'if you are the Son of God'. The suggestion made is that Jesus *can* test these possibilities should he wish to do so but by doing so he would in fact be giving in to devilish temptation. If he's hungry why not conjure up bread? If he wants to save himself why not jump so that angels can catch him to show he is the Son of God? Jesus' weary replies to the Devil indicate that he has learnt what the Israelites in the wilderness failed to – that human salvation depends on more than just food and water, and that God is to be obeyed and trusted, not tested. The third temptation is the world on a plate at a bargain condition, a switch of loyalty from God to the Devil. Not everyone has been able to resist such a temptation to rule the world.

The public ministry of Jesus

The accounts of public activity by Jesus within the gospels of Matthew, Mark and Luke fall roughly into two parts: a time of popularity in Galilee followed by a journey into Jerusalem at Passover. After some days teaching in the temple courts, Jesus is arrested one night and executed the following day. In John's Gospel, we find a different pattern. Jesus' ministry in Galilee is punctuated by trips to Jerusalem and back before travelling there for the last time. All stories are selective and we consider why the gospel writers have made their particular choices at the end of this chapter. It is useful to note at this point that some of John's information helps to clarify what would otherwise be very hard to understand. For example, according to Matthew and Mark, one of the earliest things Jesus does is to call four fishermen to follow him. They drop their nets and set off. John, however, indicates that at least two of them had already spent a day with Jesus.

The public hear that another man has taken over the role of John the Baptist, now imprisoned by Herod. Jesus arrives announcing the same message: that the time of waiting is over, that God's sovereign power is about to be unleashed on the world, and that people should be prepared for it. Jesus does more than simply talk about the sovereign power of God; he begins to exercise it, expelling evil spirits, healing the sick and controlling a storm over the lake of Galilee. It is important to notice how the people respond to such remarkable events. In the synagogue at Capernaum, they are amazed and news about him spreads rapidly. The disciples themselves are nonplussed by the calming of the storm but ask each other who *is* this person on the boat with them. Jesus himself not only talks about the sovereign power of God, he uses it. This is one explanation of his popularity.

The other reason people gather to see Jesus is to hear what he has to say. He speaks about the kingdom of God as a community who recognize God as their king. What he declares is either bound to offend some of his listeners or sound like incendiary talk to others. After all, Caesar is the temporal king and therefore it is impossible to serve two masters within one empire. Jesus speaks about this new kingdom through parables – stories which work like riddles until the moral of the story is explained. In one story, a man is sowing seed by hand on different kinds of soil and Jesus warns that not everyone will understand his teaching. Much depends on whether one is prepared to receive it. He also adds that this new kingdom is both in the present and future. The parables invite the people to accept God as their king and enter the Kingdom of Heaven but not all those invited will accept the invitation.

The call to enter the kingdom is the same as the call to be a disciple of Jesus and the cost is too great for some people. A rich man asks Jesus what he has to do. Jesus tells him to keep the Commandments. He says he has done this since he was young so Jesus asks him to go and sell all of his possessions and distribute the money among the poor. For him, it is too high a price and he goes away saddened. Jesus declares that the gain is priceless and worth everything. To make his point more forcibly, he relates two stories: one about a man who discovers treasure hidden in a field and goes and sells all he has to buy the field; the other about a merchant who finds a great pearl and sells everything he owns to purchase it.

The challenge of Jesus
Jesus undoubtedly divides people from early on in his public ministry. When he arrives in his hometown of Nazareth, and is invited

to read in the synagogue, initial admiration quickly changes to murderous rage. He points out that historically prophets have never been accepted in their own country. Some of his claims go too far for those in positions of power. When four friends lower a paralyzed man through the roof before of him, Jesus' first words to the man are that his sins are forgiven. This naturally offends the experts of Jewish Law who are present for he seems to be taking on the role of God. They bitterly criticize Jesus for fraternizing with tax collectors and prostitutes and announcing that they '[would] enter the Kingdom of God before [others]'. Jesus here appears to be undermining the elders' teachings about Sabbath observance and oral law. It is interesting to note his principles at work in each case. He argues that the Sabbath was instituted for the benefit of people, not the other way round, and that what corrupts human life is not what people eat but what comes out of their hearts and their mouths. In the Sermon on the Mount, far from relaxing the demands of the Law, Jesus seems to intensify them, so that murder and adultery are not only restricted to actions but extended to attitudes. There are many reasons therefore why people find the words of Jesus hard to hear and he himself appreciates how difficult it is to enter God's Kingdom and live in accordance with its values.

But some people are ready to follow Jesus. They include more than the first four fishermen. A tax collector and a revolutionary are also among the twelve chosen by Jesus, perhaps as the nucleus of a new Israel, for the number twelve would have reminded many of the tribes of Israel. What did someone who worked for the authorities and someone who worked against them have to say to each other around the fire in the evenings? Jesus sends all his disciples on a training mission. There are some women who accompany Jesus, too. But not all his followers leave their homes. Some, like Martha and Mary, put their homes at Jesus' disposal.

His teaching

In the Sermon on the Mount (Matthew, Chapters 5–7), Jesus teaches his disciples what kind of people they should aim to be as members of God's Kingdom. This amounts to a revolutionary challenge in the face of the existing power structures and has been appropriately described as 'the upside-down kingdom'. Followers of Jesus will inevitably be persecuted as beacons of the kingdom pointing others to God. Their response to those who treat them badly is to represent a generous expression of love, like that of God himself.

Jesus tells his disciples that God the King is also their Father. As Professor T. W. Manson wrote long ago: 'Jesus did not preach in public about the Fatherhood of God, but occasionally spoke privately about it to his closest friends and followers. For them,

---

**THE LORD'S PRAYER
(NEW LIVING TRANSLATION)**

*Our Father in Heaven,
may your name be honoured.
May your kingdom come soon.
May your will be done here on earth,
just as it is in Heaven.
Give us our food for today,
and forgive us our sins,
just as we have forgiven those
who have sinned against us.
And don't let us yield to temptation,
but deliver us from the evil one.*

Some manuscripts add:
*For yours is the kingdom
the power
and the glory forever.
Amen*

he made God the Father real, not by argument or by much speaking, but because it was obvious that the Father was the supreme reality in his own life' (p. 102). Jesus' teaching about God as Father is summarized in the Lord's Prayer (see opposite). God the Father is addressed as the King of the Kingdom, and although His coming in full glory might lie in the future, he is undeniably the one who supplies to the daily needs for bread, forgiveness and deliverance of His people. The disciples frequently fail to grasp what Jesus means although the four gospel writers do agree that clarity does come after the Resurrection has taken place.

The turning point

A major turning point in the Apostles' relationship with Jesus occurs when he takes them to the region of Caesarea Philippi in the north of Judea, near the source of the River Jordan. Here he asks them what people are saying about him and they give various replies. Herod Antipas, who has just had John the Baptist executed, superstitiously believes that John has returned from the dead. Other rumours hint that Jesus is the prophet Elijah (see p. 28). At the time, many Jews were expecting the Prophet Elijah to arrive before God's great intervention and rescue His people, and maybe Jesus is one of these other prophets. Jesus asks his Apostles: 'Who do you say I am?' and Peter gives his famous reply, 'You are the Messiah', that is, God's anointed agent, the one to act on behalf of God at the climax of history. Jesus praises this reply as a divinely given insight, but then, to their consternation, begins to speak about his imminent suffering, death and Resurrection, a message which baffles all twelve. Jesus indicates that discipleship calls for a similar willingness to self-sacrifice: death before glory.

The last journey to Jerusalem

With this message ringing in their ears, they begin the long journey back to Jerusalem. Luke's Gospel has a long journey section in the middle during which Jesus teaches, sends out a larger group of disciples on a training mission, and meets a number of varied characters on the way. He teaches both the stern demands but also the privileges of discipleship. He warns them that critical days lie ahead. Among the characters he encounters is an expert in Jewish law who knows the answer to his own question about what he must do to inherit eternal life. Jesus also stays with Mary and Martha and accepts the hospitality of a Pharisee, at whose table he gives a strongly worded criticism of their lifestyle. He heals a woman, a man with dropsy and ten lepers. This journey includes some of Jesus' most famous parables: the rich fool; the great supper; the lost sheep; the lost coin; the prodigal son; the unjust steward; the rich man and Lazarus; the unjust judge and the Pharisee and the tax collector. Anyone who takes the time to read through these challenging stories in the middle chapters of Luke's Gospel will be surprised by how many are focused on the role that wealth plays in a person's life. As Jesus declares in the Sermon on the Mount, the life of a disciple can be free from anxiety but that disciple must not compromise his position by trying to serve two masters, God and money, at once. This is a choice and a challenge.

The last week

The last week of Jesus' life in Jerusalem is covered in all of the Gospels in more detail than any of the previous three years. It begins with two public demonstrations: his dramatic entry into the city riding on a young donkey at the head of a procession and his shouting praise to God for the coming 'kingdom of our father David'. At Passover, when all Jews recall the greatest deliverance in the history of their people from slavery in Egypt, such a demonstration would have been laden with political and revolutionary overtones. To make matters worse, Jesus enters the temple and causes a flurry among those selling and buying lambs for the Passover sacrifices. He overturns the tables of usurers who are exchanging imperial Roman coins into temple money for the payment of temple tax. He denounces the authorities for turning what should have been a house of prayer into a nest of terrorists, words which echo the prophet Jeremiah's prediction of the coming destruction of the temple in his day (7:11–14). That Jesus knows the destruction of the temple is imminent is clear from his words when the disciples comment on its beautiful buildings. 'Do you see these great buildings?' Jesus asks. 'There will not be left here one stone upon another that will not be overthrown.' Such destruction is also foreshadowed by his tears when the city first comes into sight on this trip. Such public protest makes the religious authorities decide he must be destroyed. Their only problem is how to go about it when so many people seem captivated by him.

What follows is a sequence of events scarcely imaginable. The day following the demonstrations, Jesus is in the temple once more, where he is challenged by different groups of religious leaders. They ask questions designed to catch him out, discredit his answers and threaten to denounce him to the Roman authorities. But the counterquestioning and Jesus' use of the parable of the vineyard tenants to plainly indict these men (Mark 12) seem to give him the upper hand. His criticism of the Pharisees is forthright and direct. But, once again, this calls up the shadow of grief. Outside the temple, Jesus speaks of its destruction to his disciples and the troubles which will accompany these events. He also mentions his future coming as the Son of Man, an expression found in Daniel 7 for one who receives the Kingdom on behalf of the people of God. God knows when this will be (evidently in the future) and Jesus has taught his disciples to prepare by praying.

Then, just as the authorities have decided to postpone dealing with Jesus until after the Passover festival, one of his closest disciples, Judas Iscariot, betrays him into their hands, away from the crowds. Jesus shares one last meal with his disciples, during which he speaks about a day in the future when he will drink wine in the Kingdom of God. Jesus and his Apostles make their way to the garden of Gethsemane, where three disciples stay awake long enough to hear Jesus pray to God his Father and ask whether he might possibly be spared his coming ordeal. At the same time, he commits himself to His Father's Will. He is arrested in this garden at daybreak and taken away to the house of the high priest. Most of the disciples desert Jesus at this point in spite of their previousy brave words. Peter follows Jesus into the court-yard of the house of the high priest, where he denies he ever had anything to do with Jesus, twice to a servant girl and once to a bystander who recognizes his Galilean accent.

The high priest questions Jesus point-blank about whether he is indeed the Messiah. Jesus replies that he is and how one day he will be seated at God's right hand. This leads to a denuncia-tion for blasphemy and a call for his death. To get such a sentence carried out, the Jewish authorities try to persuade Pontius Pilate, the Roman governor, that Jesus is guilty of the political charge of claiming to be a king and a rival of Caesar. Pilate is unconvinced but naively offers Jesus to the Jews as the prisoner to be released that Passover. The fickle crowds ask that Barabbas' life be spared, even though he is a real criminal, and Pilate finds his hand forced in condemning Jesus to his crucifixion. Jesus' death is movingly told (Mark 15:22–41). Death is certified by the centurion in charge of the execution squad and Pilate releases the body for burial.

Why *was* Jesus crucified? We have observed tension between him and the religious leaders escalate over the course of three years. Jesus' radical interpretation of Jewish law has also caused offence and bypassed the debates of the elders. His talk of a kingdom in Heaven and his popularity with the 'people of the land' have made the Jewish authorities nervous about political unrest which would threaten the status quo. They fear Jesus will act as a catalyst in bringing about the Roman destruction he sometimes seems to forecast.

Not the end

But this, the Gospels say, is not the end. Of all the remarkable and earth-shattering events in relation to Jesus that week, the Gospels end with accounts of an empty tomb and the disciples encountering Jesus in a resurrected state. All four Gospels present this incredible event in a sequence of stories told with remarkable restraint. Starting with Mark 16:1–8, we have an impossible account: most scholars think the gospel finishes with verse 8 but logic shows that it cannot possibly have done. If it had, then no one would ever have known about the Resurrection! Inevitably the women must have gone out and told their menfolk stories of these various encounters which filled out the main narrative. It transforms the disciples into individuals willing to lay down their lives for their faith. One of the most persuasive stories is told by Luke in his last chapter. A reading of this account, full of intense realism and humanity, has persuaded many of the truthfulness of its message. Luke follows this with a last seminar from Jesus for the disciples. He teaches them that the Old Testament Scriptures explain the necessity for his 'mortal' death, a rather novel explanation. Jesus also commissions the Apostles to take and impart the message of forgiveness to all nations.

Thus this is the way in which the four Gospels bear witness to the story of Jesus. We now turn from the general story to a more detailed appreciation of the specific flavour that each Gospel lends the story. They will be discussed in the order in which they are presented in the New Testament.

DISTINCTIVE FEATURES OF MATTHEW

The beginning

Matthew opens his account with a dramatic overture that declares his story to be about a new beginning. His first four words talk about 'the genesis of Jesus Christ' in contrast to the Book of Genesis at the beginning of the Bible. This declaration is followed by a long list of people's names most of them unknown, and the reason for the list seems obscure at first. But Matthew gives us a clue in 1:17: he explains that he has artificially constructed the genealogy in three groups with fourteen names in each group. Since Hebrew consonant letters were also used for numbers, and the letters of David's name add up to fourteen, these opening verses are like a flashing neon sign headed by 'the genesis of Jesus Christ, son of David'. They sketch the history of Israel from Abraham to David, from David to the exile, and from the exile to 'the Christ' or Messiah. The Messiah is God's anointed agent or king and many Jews at this time are longing for the arrival of a real Messiah, a king like David, who will restore freedom and prosperity to Israel. In the following chapter in Matthew, the magi ask about this newborn king of the Jews. Herod, temporal king of the Jews, takes steps to safeguard his throne against a possible political rival. Later on in the story, which all of the Gospels relate, Jesus rides into Jerusalem acclaimed as king. This presages the chilling inscription ('King of the Jews') that will be nailed on his Cross.

Matthew's title verse also declares Jesus Christ to be the 'son of Abraham'. If we turn to the last few verses of Matthew's Gospel, we find that Jesus tells his disciples to go and make disciples of all nations. This suggests that calling Jesus the 'son of Abraham' is not just saying he is a true Jew and a member of Israel, but that he is the direct descendant of Abraham, through whom all nations of the world will be blessed. Matthew begins by announcing a new creation through Jesus Christ, the long-awaited Messiah and son of Abraham, who will bring God's blessing to the world.

Matthew goes on to indicate that Jesus is unique through the story of his conception. When Joseph realizes that Mary, his bride-to-be, is already pregnant, he thinks it might be better to call off the wedding altogether. This introduces to us an unusual feature in these birth stories – the role of dreams as a means of receiving messages from God. Joseph is informed that this conception is 'immaculate', the work of the Holy Spirit, Giver of Life. This event is a new genesis for the Spirit of God which also created the world.

Matthew is well placed at the beginning of the New Testament with his outline of God's plan in the Old Testament. The birth stories which he tells are punctuated with quotations from the Old Testament Scriptures in the form of editorial comments. They proclaim that this child was anticipated or promised in those very scriptures. Jesus' birth is therefore evidence that God has not deserted His people. Not only will He save His people, the Jews, but He will be acknowledged by all the nations of the world. This is probably the significance behind the story of the three magi. Jesus is recognized and worshipped by representatives of different nations while Herod, the temporal king, seeks his extermination.

The teacher

When the public ministry of Jesus begins, Matthew presents him as the teacher, dividing much of Jesus' teachings into five sections: the Sermon on the Mount (5–7); instructions about mission (10:5–11:1); parables of the kingdom (13); life in the Church (18); and the future (24–25).

What is the content of Jesus' teaching? The theme of the Sermon is the way of life that is expected of Jesus' disciples – a 'righteousness' that goes beyond that of the experts of the Law and the Pharisees. 'Righteousness' means living a life that is right for people belonging to God and to each other in a covenant that recognizes God as their king. The fact that Jesus assumes he knows all of this, and has the right to teach it, says something about what he thought of himself so it is not surprising to read that the crowds were astonished. The instructions about mission were evidently to be useful not just for the initial training sessions while Jesus was still with the Apostles, but also for when they came to carry out his final mission. Similarly, teaching about life in the Church and the future suggests that Jesus is still looking ahead for the life of the world to come.

Matthew has a significant extension of the conversation between Jesus and Peter at Caesarea Philippi when he speaks of building his Church on people like Peter. This outlook to his teaching is in keeping with the fact that, while the Kingdom of God is at work within him, the full coming of the kingdom still lies in the future.

Jesus teaches that he will come again and speaks of himself in terms of the Son of Man. Earlier in the Gospel, he used that phrase to mean 'someone like me'. For example, he claims the authority to forgive sins and describes his way of life as that of someone with no fixed abode. His words recall that of a figure found in Daniel 7, where the writer sees 'someone like a son of man' to whom God has given eternal sovereign authority. Jesus speaks of exercising that same authority when judging 'all the nations'. The outcome of this judgment be surprising for many: some will be welcomed into the kingdom and others will be banished. The grounds for this judgment will be the ways in which people have treated others, for in dealing with them Jesus declares that they have been dealing with him.

Matthew's reasons

Why *did* Matthew present the gospel in this way? When Jesus sent the twelve out on their mission, he instructed them not to go to the gentiles or the Samaritans but only to the Jews. He also told a Canaanite woman that he had been sent to the Jews only. Yet the gentile mission is foreshadowed in the story of the magi and is the subject of the final commission. It may well have been that historically Jesus' mission was directed first at the Jews and later to gentiles through the disciples. Paul tells the Christians in Rome that this is his policy [Romans, 1:16] but it is also reasonable to suppose that Matthew is writing:

- for churches in which there are significant numbers of Jewish Christians concerned about how the gospel relates to their Jewish heritage. Matthew shows them how their Christian faith is a continuation of their Jewish faith but he transposes it into a different key with new features.

- At the same time, there are gentile Christians in these churches who need to respect the Jewish roots of their faith while still recognizing they are now engaged in a global mission.

DISTINCTIVE FEATURES OF MARK

Who is this man?

Mark's Gospel has no birth stories in it but opens with a prologue which lets his readers into secrets of what is going on but which are hidden from the characters that we meet in his story. His prologue tells us this is the story of Jesus the Messiah (Christ) who is also the Son of God. The significance of these names becomes much clearer as the story unfolds. That Jesus is 'the Christ' is not recognized until 8:29. After that, Jesus refers to his followers as disciples of Christ and sets the Jewish experts a riddle about 'the Christ', warning against false Messiahs. When the high priest interrogates him at his trial, Jesus accepts that he *is* the Christ. He is also recognized as the 'son of David', enters Jerusalem as a king, and is executed under the title 'King of the Jews'. It is interesting that Jesus is repeatedly recognized as the Son of God: first, by the supernatural testimony of demons; second, by the voice from Heaven; and third, by the centurion at the Cross. These events all probably mean different things to different eyewitnesses. For Mark, this probably meant that Jesus could indeed walk on water, exercise a divine right over the forgiveness of sins, and be able to claim eternal significance for his teachings. John the Baptist is part of the prologue for he is in prison when the main action of the Gospel unfolds. John fulfils prophecies about there being messenger who prefigures the coming of the Lord himself. In these ways, Mark portrays Jesus as the one who fulfils Jewish hopes.

Jesus' remarkable authority and dynamic personality are evident from the way he can call upon people to be his disciples and they will abandon everything to follow him, forming the nucleus of the messianic community. Yet those people who wish to charge him with blasphemy are also threatening to kill him. Above all, there is no doubt that Jesus is human by the way in which he responds to situations which grieve him, his need for sleep, the reactions by people who know him well, his limitations, and his anxiety in preparation for his ordeal.

Mark's Gospel is centred on the Cross. A real threat already looms judging from the fate of John the Baptist. As early as Chapter 3:6, unlikely partners are plotting to kill Jesus. After Peter's recognition of Jesus as the Messiah, Jesus repeatedly warns his disciples about his coming Passion and hints at an eventual explanation for all this pain. But this is something the disciples cannot yet understand. When on trial before the high priest, various false charges are presented regarding the destruction and the rebuilding of the temple. The high priest asks Jesus: 'Are you the Messiah, the son of God?' An affirmative answer leads to his condemnation.

Mark's reasons

The Gospel according to Mark is probably written following a time of persecution and we can surmise that part of its purpose is:

- to reassure Christians that those who suffer death itself are following their Lord.

- He may also intend to challenge those who are reticent to confess their faith and encourage those who do not understand or have failed. The portrait of Peter is an encouragement to any would-be disciple. Here is one who often does not understand Jesus and denies his Master three times yet Jesus does not write him off (see 16:7).

- It is sometimes said that Mark wants to correct the false picture of Jesus as a worker of wonders. True, he performs remarkable miracles but the shadow of the Cross is there almost from the beginning. That Jesus is crucified is an integral part of his mission, not a tragic end, as Jesus tries to explain.

DISTINCTIVE FEATURES OF LUKE

Birth and boyhood

Luke also shows that Jesus is the promised Messiah through his version of the birth stories. Angels, the messengers of God, also play significant roles. When the Angel tells Mary she is to bear a son, Jesus, he prophecizes that 'he will be great, and will be called the Son of the Most High; and the Lord God will give to him the throne of his father, David, he will reign over the House of Jacob forever; and of his kingdom there will be no end'. These words echo great prophetic promises. When the Christ Child is born in Bethlehem, the city of David, the angels inform the shepherds thus: 'to you is born this day in the city of David, a Saviour, who is Christ the Lord'. This message is politically subversive for the one Lord and Saviour within the Roman world at the time would have been the emperor.

Jesus is circumcised in accordance with Jewish law. An old man and woman, Simeon and Anna, both of whom see Jesus as the key to Israel's salvation, repeat the message proclaimed by the angels at Jesus' birth. When the circumcision celebrations are over, the family return to Nazareth, the city of Mary and Joseph. There is also an anecdote from Jesus' childhood when, at the age of twelve, he is taken to Jerusalem for the first time and lingers on in the temple, calling it his father's house.

The prophet and Saviour

Luke's portrait of Jesus identifies him as a prophet as well as the Messiah and Saviour. A prophet in the Bible is primarily someone who speaks or acts on behalf of God. At the synagogue in Nazareth, Jesus claims that he is the prophet Isaiah had spoken about but he goes on to say that 'no prophet is accepted in his own country'. The congregation shows the reality of this by threatening to kill Jesus. Jesus later identifies himself as a prophet who must perish in Jerusalem.

Jesus tells the tax collector Zacchaeus he has come 'to seek and save the lost', and he defends his keeping company with 'tax collectors and sinners' by relating three parables about the joys of finding what has been lost. In 22:37 he identifies himself with the suffering servant of Isaiah 53:12. In the context of the whole of Isaiah 52:13–53:12, we have a rich source for pondering on how Jesus understood his coming death. The offer of Paradise to the repentant thief dying on the Cross next to Jesus illustrates his ability to give life even as he breathes his last. The explanation comes after the Resurrection. In Luke's last chapter, Jesus repeatedly explains that his death was an integral part of God's plan as foretold in the Scriptures.

Luke's reasons

Luke specifically indicates his reasons for writing his gospel.

- He intends to strengthen the faith of Theophilus, possibly his wealthy patron, as one example of a person in official circles who has become a Christian. Luke may have had such wealthy people in mind. If this conjecture is right, it makes the warnings about the dangers of wealth particularly interesting.
- Perhaps the church audiences of gentiles are also in view and Luke intends to reassure them that they, too, are included in God's people.

DISTINCTIVE FEATURES OF JOHN

The prologue

John's Gospel is in a different key. He opens with a majestic prologue which is read out in most carol services at Christmas. As with Mark's Gospel, we must remember that the prologue is only presented for the reader's benefit and that the characters in the story are not privy to it. The prologue begins by drawing attention to the Word of God, which is separate from God yet also intrinsic to Him – God's self-expression as it were. As the Book of Genesis shows, the Word of God is the means by which He created the world. Now, John says, the Word of God is expressed in a human form and the invisible God can be seen in his Son, identified with Jesus Christ. This becomes one of the major themes of this Gospel – Jesus as the Son of God who makes God the Father known, because everything he does and teaches is what God has made known to him. Like Father, like Son. Jesus was sent by the Father into this world to save people from destruction and give them life.

To those who believe in him, God gives the right to make a new start within God's own family. This is to share in the life of God himself, the 'eternal life', the life of the kingdom, a new creation of the Spirit of God.

The two books

The fourth Gospel is in two main parts: the Book of Signs (Chapters 1–12), followed by the Book of the Passion, which is actually a glorious revelation of the extent to which God is prepared to rescue His people (Chapters 13–21). The signs, as the miracles are called, are illustrations of the eternal life that Jesus embodies. At the wedding at Cana, he transforms water into wine – an indication of the quality of the new life. This and the miracle of the feeding of the 5,000 provide hints of the heavenly banquet of Jewish hopes. Several signs show that this new life will replace sickness, blindness and death itself. They point to the great work which Jesus himself is accomplishing through his death and Resurrection. John the Baptist announces this in the first chapter in his testimony. Twice he says, 'Look, the Lamb of God', pointing to Jesus, and the first time he adds 'who takes away the sins of the world'. Lambs taking away sins within a Jewish context would have reminded people about the sacrifices being offered up in the temple. At Passover, they would also recall the Exodus from Egypt for roast lamb was eaten during the Passover meal. Jesus speaks about the necessity for the son of Man to be lifted up, like the bronze serpent Moses lifts up onto a pole in an Old Testament story, as a means of saving the Jewish people from deadly bites in the wilderness. Jesus describes his role as that of the good shepherd laying down his life for his sheep. Certainly when John comes to tell the story of Jesus' arrest, trial and Crucifixion, he portrays Jesus much more in charge of the proceedings, even questioning the Roman governor. On the Cross, he expresses concern for his mother after he is gone and dies with a one-word cry: that his mission is finished. After the Resurrection, Jesus comforts Mary, commissions the disciples to continue his work, confronts doubting Thomas and forgives Peter in an unforgettable episode.

John's reasons

Like Luke, John tells us why he selected what he chooses to tell us about Jesus (20:30–31) in his Gospel.

- John either intends for his Gospel to bring people to faith in Jesus the Messiah, Son of God
- or that it will encourage them to continue in the faith they already hold. His Gospel is used for both purposes.
- Perhaps he also writes to reassure Jewish Christians in the face of criticism and opposition from non-Christian Jews. One of the striking themes here is that Jesus himself fulfils what Jewish rituals and festivals pointed towards, and that through coming to know Jesus, through his Spirit, one comes to know God himself.

This sketch of the story of the gospel and the four complementary portraits of Jesus that are presented in them indicate the definitive 'authorized version' that is officially recognized by the Church in terms of its teachings. These gospel accounts are the subject of much later thinking, painting, drama and writing in an attempt to clarify and apply them to the daily lives of those who acknowledge Jesus as their Lord.

Chapter 3

Jesus and the first Christians

The name 'Christians' was first given to followers of Jesus at Antioch in Syria. They had previously been known as disciples or believers, those who belonged to the Way as taught by Jesus. A church was established at Antioch by fugitives from Jerusalem escaping persecution and some of them were the first to share their faith with local Greek-speaking gentiles. Their message can be summed up as 'Jesus is Lord'. We will explore what this means below. The church at Jerusalem had sent Barnabas to report on what was happening. He encouraged the Church and spent a year teaching these 'Christians'. Presumably those in the church at Antioch were called thus because they were always speaking about Christ or following the Way of Christ.

There are two key questions for us to address at this point. How did these first Christians talk about Jesus to people outside of their communities, and how did they discuss Jesus amongst themselves?

HOW DID THE FIRST CHRISTIANS SPEAK TO OUTSIDERS ABOUT JESUS?

We now turn to the Book of Acts. From the way this book opens, it is evident it was the second of two volumes written by Luke to Theophilus, his friend and patron. Since he claims that his former book (Luke's Gospel) was written about what Jesus began to do and teach, he implies that this is just what Jesus continued to do. This is confirmed in the narrative of Acts when, for example, Peter tells a bed-ridden man: 'Aeneas, Jesus Christ heals you' and he gets up. This might seem strange in that both Luke's Gospel and the opening chapter of the Acts give a dramatic account of Jesus' last meeting with the disciples. They understand he had been taken to Heaven to God yet how can he be still be present among them? Although scholars are reluctant to borrow ideas from another New Testament writer to explain Luke's thinking, it makes sense to suppose that, like John, he also understood the Holy Spirit to be the means through which Jesus could be present and working through them. Certainly before he left, Jesus had spoken about the gift of the Holy Spirit, and Peter explained that the product of this was what had happened to the Christ on the day of Pentecost. It is the Holy Spirit who empowers the Apostles to act 'in the name of Jesus' as his authorized representatives and Luke says that 'the Spirit of Jesus' is directed at Paul and his fellows on their travels. We, too, should revise our ideas about Heaven because although the disciples had seen Jesus go, and heard him promise he would return, Jesus in the meantime had still spoken directly to other people according to the Book of Acts. Perhaps Heaven is a dimension of our present experience of which we are seldom aware.

Speeches in the Book of Acts

To explore how Christians spoke to outsiders about Jesus, we must turn to those speeches where they express their opinions of Christ and his significance to them. Most of the speeches here are attributed to Peter and Paul but there is one notable speech by Stephen, the first Christian martyr. When we take a look at these accounts, it is clear the speakers must have said much more than what we are told and that what we actually have are just brief summaries. There has been considerable debate about the genuine reliability of such summaries. It has been suggested Luke followed the example of Thucydides in his *History of the Peloponnesian War* (5th century BCE). He wrote:

> As to the speeches, which were made either before or during the war, it is hard for me, and for others who reported them to me, to recollect the exact words. I have therefore put into the mouth of each speaker the sentiments proper to the occasion, expressed as I thought he would be likely to have expressed them, while at the same time I endeavour, as nearly as I can to give the general import of what was actually said.

One can imagine ludicrous pictures of people in the middle of a battle trying to take notes on what the commanding officers are saying. It is much more likely that someone simply recalled the essence of what was said afterwards. When applied to the Book of Acts, this can be read in several ways, but the fact Luke gives reliable summaries is suggested by a lack of stylistic flourishes and the differences between the speeches addressed to different audiences. We may therefore assume that we have the general gist of what was said in a summarized form.

Peter's speeches

The first major speech addressed to outsiders is Peter's explanation of the rather extraordinary events surrounding the Feast of Pentecost, fifty days after the Crucifixion and Resurrection of Jesus (Acts 2). Crowds are always in Jerusalem for three of the most important festival days of the Jewish calendar: Passover, Pentecost and Tabernacles. That particular year in 33 CE, they experience something rather different. They overhear a group of Galileans speaking about what God has done and, though the speakers are Galileans, the crowds hear them utter their own native languages, despite the fact they come from different parts of the Roman Empire. Most are amazed. Some of them joke that the Galileans are drunk. Peter stands up to explain. He says it is all due to 'Jesus of Nazareth, a man God publicly endorsed'. This declaration underlines that Jesus is a human being from a specific geographical location. Peter adds that God has given them evidence that Jesus is indeed someone special by working miracles through him. Then comes the bombshell when Peter claims Jesus has been handed over to be killed as part of God's own design. This is extraordinary, especially as it was widely believed that someone who was crucified was under God's curse. Where did Peter get this idea about God's plan from? It can only have been from Jesus himself and his explanation of the divine necessity of his death in terms of the Old Testament Scriptures. But Peter does not stop here. He goes on to illustrate the claim that God has raised Jesus from the dead in accordance with the

Scriptures and to say that Jesus now shares God's executive authority and sovereign rule. The gift of the Holy Spirit, which explains the extraordinary events of that day, is now here in the figure of Jesus Christ.

It is not difficult to see how 'out of this world' such an explanation would be to people today who can give no content to words like 'God' or 'his kingdom' and can at best only vaguely imagine something like the 'Spirit'. But the impact on that day was tremendous for 3,000 people accepted the truth of Peter's words and hailed Jesus as the Lord and the Messiah. For Christians, calling Jesus 'Lord' meant that he had absolute authority over them as their master and they owed him absolute obedience. Peter gives similar explanations in the temple following the healing of a lame man (Acts 3–4). In these speeches there are echoes of the prophecy of Isaiah (52:13–53:12) because Jesus is called God's servant and references are made to his glorious exaltation after heart-breaking mortal suffering. Reading the song in Isaiah helps to fill in the developing picture of how Peter and the rest of the Apostles understood God's plan and Jesus' death. Peter goes on to speak about God who will be sending Jesus back again in the future, at the end of time. The number of those who decide to convert is now 5,000.

In a third speech, Peter addresses gentiles from the house of Cornelius, the Roman centurion (Acts 10). They are pious, God-fearing people who pray and give money to the poor. Peter acknowledges that God does not pick favourites and proclaims that Jesus Christ is 'Lord of all'. His speech is notable due the gospel story outline it gives, which is very similar to Mark's Gospel – not surprisingly Mark was later to write down Peter's preaching onto papyrus. Peter adds that God has appointed Jesus to be the

the ultimate judge of all humankind and that everyone who believes in him will be forgiven rather than condemned on Judgment Day. The atmosphere is charged with the powerful manifestation of God's Spirit, which compels these gentiles to praise God. Peter instructs them to be baptized in the name of Jesus Christ. This Christian baptism goes further than that of John the Baptist as it indicates the end of their former way of life and marks their new beginning as people of Christ. During baptism, Christians acknowledge Jesus as their Lord and commit themselves to serving him.

Stephen's speech

Stephen gives a more aggressive speech (Acts 7) when he is on trial himself. He argues that what has happened to Jesus is the climax of a long history of disobedience by the people of God, who effectively have 'murdered' the Righteous One. He claims to see Jesus in Heaven seated at the right-hand of the Father. This is too much for the Jewish crowd who stone him to death. He dies forgiving them as Jesus forgives those who crucified him. Saul of Tarsus, one of the witnesses, then begins a systematic attempt to persecute the Christian churches in Jerusalem and further afield.

WHO WAS SAUL?

Saul was the Jewish name of the man who we know better as Paul (his Greek name). In his letter to the church at Philippi, he recounts a fragment of his life by describing himself as a true Jew 'circumcised on the eighth day, a member of the people of Israel, of the tribe of Benjamin, a Hebrew born of Hebrews; as to the law, a Pharisee; as to zeal, a persecutor of the Church; as to righteousness under the law, blameless'. That he was of the tribe of Benjamin shows that he was from that small yet distinguished tribe from which Saul, the first king of Israel, had come. That he was a Pharisee demonstrates he was one of that small minority of people particularly keen on keeping and teaching the Law. We met them in our first chapter. The third notable thing Paul tells us here is that he is a persecutor of the Church. The Book of Acts gives us more information on this aspect of Paul's career.

Why did he persecute Christians so fiercely? The religious leaders had secured the execution of Jesus and he had been crucified (hung on an artificial tree). According to Jewish law, it was stated that anyone hung on a tree was under God's curse and it was obviously impossible for Jesus to be both cursed by God and, at the same time, the chosen Messiah. Not only were these Christians threatening to undermine the authority of the Jewish leaders, but they were blaspheming against God and in danger of being as guilty as Jesus. It was urgent to literally shut them up for they would not be able to spread their lies any further in prison.

However, the account in Acts 9 relates that, as Paul approaches Damascus, he is literally knocked over by a blinding encounter with the risen Jesus. This is one of the most famous conversion stories of all time and people still talk about someone having 'a Damascus road experience.' Jesus addresses him and asks him why Paul is persecuting him. Paul learns three striking lessons from that encounter. First, he realizes that Jesus is alive, incredible as that must seem to him. Second, he learns that Jesus is 'in glory' having been promoted into the presence of God. He is no longer under God's curse but has indeed become one with God. Third, and equally strangely, he begins to understand that Jesus somehow identifies with his followers. He is too overwhelmed to reply to Jesus but he might have thought that he was persecuting Jesus and not his followers. But Jesus had said 'persecuting me'. Paul later writes to the Galatians that God has revealed his Son 'in me' and, in a letter to the Church at Corinth, he comments that 'for it is the God who said "Let light shine out of darkness" who has shone in our hearts to give the light of the knowledge of the glory of God in the face of Jesus Christ.' This seems to be reminiscent of the experience on the road to Damascus and suggests that to Paul it must have felt like an act of creation. From that point on, he certainly sees Jesus and everything else in a different light. Following his conversion, he begins to proclaim in synagogues that Jesus really is the Son of God, a title which at first might have been an alternative name for 'the Messiah'. However, a reflection on the vision he has had soon enlarges the significance of the phrase 'the Son of God'.

HOW DID PAUL SPEAK TO OUTSIDERS?

There are speeches by Paul, both in a Jewish context at the synagogue of Antioch in the province of Pisidia (Acts 13), and in more gentile contexts, at Lystra (Acts 14) and Athens (Acts 17), where he could not take Jewish suppositions for granted.

To Jewish audiences

On the day of the Sabbath, Paul and his friends are invited to address the congregation at Antioch, following the reading from the Law and the Prophets. It is Paul who responds by giving a plotted outline of the history of God's dealings with his people from the time of the exodus from Egypt to King David. From David, he jumps straight

to Jesus, the promised Saviour, saying that the news of this salvation is for meant for them, his listeners. He recounts how religious
leaders in Jerusalem condemned Jesus to death by handing him over
to the Roman governor for execution because they did not understand the Scriptures. After Jesus' death and burial, God raised him
into the heavens to sit at his right, and for some weeks, he appeared
to those who would then bear witness to these great truths. Paul
concludes with an offer of forgiveness and a warning not to reject
God's message. The meeting breaks up with many becoming
believers and others asking them to return the next Sabbath.

To pagan audiences

What takes place at Lystra and Athens proves very different. At
Lystra, a town in the Roman province of Galatia, Paul and his
companions encounter a cripple who has never walked in his life.
He listens carefully to Paul, who tells him to stand up on his own
two feet. To everyone's surprise, he does. The crowd who has been
listening now begins to shout out that the gods Zeus and Hermes
have come. Zeus was the chief of the Greek gods and Hermes was
his messenger. They call Paul 'Hermes' because he has been doing
most of the talking. The priest of Zeus starts to make prepara-
tions to sacrifice oxen in their honour. When Barnabas and Paul
realize what is happening, they run out into the crowd to say they
are only mortal men and to tell them that 'we bring you good
news that you should turn from these worthless things to the living
God.' They describe him as the creator of everything who used to
let people go their own way but who now has given them clues
of his existence in the blessings of rain and good harvests. Paul
and his followers stop the sacrifices in the nick of time. The

intriguing question here is why did the people think Paul and Barnabas were gods and not just travelling miracle workers? There is a legend which the Greek poet Ovid tells about a visit made by Zeus and Hermes to inhabitants of this very region. On that occasion, no one gave the gods hospitality apart from an old couple, Philemon and Baucis. The gods then destroyed the town but rewarded the old couple. Perhaps when Paul and Barnabas came, the people were concerned to not repeat their ancestors' mistakes. It is interesting to see that Paul and Barnabas do not mention Jesus at all. To fully understand Jesus, it is necessary to have some grasp of the living God, the Creator and provider of daily food. Only then does it make sense to talk about God sending down his Son, and even that would need careful explanation to people from their kind of background because Zeus, too, had sons.

At Athens, Paul is waiting for his friends, Silas and Timothy, and is upset to see so many pagan statues of gods and goddesses. He talks about this idolatry in the synagogue, where no doubt he receives a sympathetic hearing, and in the marketplace where people are more inclined to harangue. He seems to have progressed beyond the point of arguing about God to speaking about Jesus and the Resurrection when some Epicurean and Stoic philosophers overhear him and think that he is talking about two gods, Jesus and Resurrection [*Anastasis*]. They arrest him and take him before the Council of the *Areopagus*. This council has full responsibility for maintaining religious custom and order in the city and can act as a court. Paul begins his speech by referring to an altar that he has seen in the city bearing the inscription, 'To the unknown god' and says he is going to now tell them about this God, who is the Creator of everything and who, as Lord of Heaven and Earth, does not need temples or people to serve him. On the contrary, he gives all people 'life and breath and everything'. This god made all the people on the face of the earth and now wants them to find him. At this point, Paul quotes two Greek poets whose words indicate that people depend on God and belong to his family. Paul does not mention Jesus by name but having said that God commands all people to repent (that is, to turn back to him), he declares that God has appointed one man to be judge on Judgment Day. As proof of this, he has raised this man from the dead. The claim divides his audience: some jeer, others say they would like to hear Paul speak again. Some convert on the spot.

It is clear that while Paul can speak of Jesus as the climax of Jewish history in the eyes of the Jews, when he speaks to gentiles with no connection to Judaism, he is first compelled to argue for the one living Creator God who has been at work in Jesus. But, even so, he stresses that God commands all people to repent because he has appointed Jesus Christ to be judge of all.

HOW DID CHRISTIANS TALK TO EACH OTHER ABOUT JESUS?

For evidence of this, we turn to the letters of Paul. His first surviving letter was probably the one written to the Galatians some time before the so-called Council of Jerusalem met in 49 CE. The last letter to which his name is attached is 2 Timothy, which was probably written in the first half of the 60s.

Few references to his public ministry

When Paul came to write about Jesus, he made few references to his life and ministry. He mentions his birth 'under the law' (Galatians 4:4), an expression which indicates that Jesus was a Jew.

Paul reminds the Christians in Rome that Jesus was 'descended from David', a necessary qualification to be the Messiah (Romans 1:3). He knows about Jesus' brothers and the fact that one of them, James, was a member of the church in Jerusalem. There are some, but not many, references to the teachings of Jesus and there is the account of the Last Supper. There are far more references to his death on the Cross and the Resurrection. It is highly probable that Paul knew more than he tells about the life and teaching of Jesus. We must remember that letters are different kinds of documents to gospels or books. Paul is here addressing people who are already Christians and what he writes would have depended on the partic-ular needs and issues arising within these churches.

Earliest Christian beliefs

At the same time, Paul's letters sometimes give us an insight into the ideas that the earliest Christians held about Jesus. If the Christ was crucified around the year 33, then Paul was converted the following year, or the year after at the very most. Sometimes he quotes the beliefs held by earlier Christians. We earlier referred to his letter to the Corinthians (15:3); in this respect, it is important to consider this verse within its entire paragraph. When Paul writes that he 'passed on' what he also 'received', he is adopting a Jewish manner of speech in handing down such significant teachings. In these verses, the teaching is a summary of the gospel which Paul himself had been taught and which he then passed on to the Corinthians. It includes four points:

- Christ died for our sins, according to the Scriptures,
- He was buried,

- He was raised on the third day, according to the Scriptures,
- He was seen by witnesses.

To this last point, Paul adds a footnote about himself. The phrase 'according to the Scriptures' recalls the speeches of Peter and of those teaching sessions by Jesus after his Resurrection when he told the disciples that the Scriptures testified to the necessity for the Messiah's death. These four points are statements of the essential Christian beliefs and teachings.

Paul may intend something similar when he refers to his teaching of the Last Supper. This, too, was something he had 'received' and 'passed on'. What is clear from Paul's preaching and teaching is his dominant theme of the Crucifixion of Christ. He acknowledges that this is a message with potentially embarrassing aspects for both Jewish and Greek audiences. To the Greeks, the Cross represents foolishness. How could a hero, a saviour figure, be of any help to anyone else when he was unable to save himself? Paul insists God has turned human ideas upside down and for those prepared to trust in Jesus and commit their lives to him, Jesus the Messiah is their life, wisdom, and salvation. This message is a stumbling-block for Jews, as it had been for Paul at first as well because a cross indicates the curse of God. After his encounter with the risen Christ on the road to Damascus, Paul had to revise his ideas. He comes to realize that Jesus had been made a curse for others so that God's promise to Abraham – that through one of his descendants all the nations of the world would be blessed – could be realized. Jesus is this descendant, so what does all this mean and how can this be?

The gospel according to Paul

Paul gives his fullest explanation in a letter to the Christians in
Rome. He begins by arguing that everyone – both Jews and gentiles
– continue to fall short of what God desires. The climax of this
statement is that people are not respecting God nor looking for
him, let alone obeying him. They are prisoners of the 'power of
sin', that inward distortion which leads to idolatry and immorality
and exposes them to God's wrath and judgment. Yet God has still
intervened on their behalf so that the situation may be rectified.

In his diagnosis of the human condition, Paul draws upon his
Jewish heritage. The Bible opens with an account of the Creation of
the world and its inhabitants, all of which are brought into being by
God's word of command. God says it is all very good but then the
story of Adam and Eve disgraces the human race (and by implica-
tion, all of Creation) from this perfect state of goodness. When Paul
turns to the remedy that is required, he employs Jewish sacrificial
ideas. Animal sacrifices are essential for maintaining a good relationship between the people and their holy, living God. Through a
number of incidents in their history, the Jews have learnt that God's
holiness can be dangerous, even fatal. Offending God by breaking
His laws, refusing to listen to his messengers, and failing to be the
people he desires, are all aspects of sin. This can only be put right
by offering a particular kind of sacrifice, a 'sin-offering'. He makes a
most astounding statement when he declares that God himself,
through the death of his Son, Jesus, has offered the sacrifice to end
all sacrifices. Normally people offer sacrifices to God but, in this
instance, it is God himself who gives us his Son as the means for
wiping out sin for good. He expresses it slightly differently elsewhere
when he says that Christ became what we are ('sin') so that we might

become what he is – 'righteous', restored to a right relationship with God. Jesus Christ takes the place of the condemned, those under the curse, that they might be forgiven and live as God's Spirit now directs. This is also what was meant by the saying 'Christ died for our sins': so that we could be reconciled with God. In Paul's Gospel, he appeals to people to accept this through faith alone and commit themselves to Jesus by serving Him in his new family of believers – those who trust him. Social differences are no longer important. While Jews might stumble over this, as Paul himself has, the message of the Cross remains central to Paul's preaching.

The Crucifixion is followed by the Resurrection and it is worth remembering here that the word 'resurrection', when applied to Jesus and to those who believe in him, does not necessarily mean that part of them does not die, merely that it continues to live on in another form. It is rather like someone dying physically but being given new spiritual life. Paul tells the Corinthians how Christian faith stands or falls by the Resurrection of Jesus Christ. For Paul this is confirmed by Christ's appearances post-Resurrection, including the one to Paul. It is the Resurrection of Jesus which holds out the promise of future resurrection for those who believe in him. Here, as in Romans 5, Paul compares Christ to Adam, who represents the whole of the human race. But there is a contrast between the two. There are those, who like Adam and Eve, have declared their independence from God and gone their own way down the path that leads to death. Those who come to trust in Christ, and live for him as their Lord, on the other hand, are set on another path, one which leads to Resurrection and to life. Paul says that one day, death and all those who oppose God, will be destroyed and Christ will hand the kingdom back to God (1 Corinthians, Chapter 15). This is the central Christian hope.

How is it that the death and Resurrection of one man is so significant for millions of people? It all depends on who he is. If an understanding of the Cross and Resurrection baffles you, then trying to grasp who Paul thinks Jesus really is will only stretch you further, and you may have to be content yourself with only a partial understanding. In his Letter to the Philippians, Paul quotes two stanzas from an early Christian hymn in which he shows that the early Christians already held incredible ideas about Jesus. He introduces this hymn because he wants to encourage the Philippians to be like Jesus and have the same humble attitude that Jesus had. The quota-

---

THE PHILIPPIAN HYMN [2:6–11, TNIV]

(Jesus) who being in very nature God,
did not consider equality with God
something to be used to his own advantage;
rather, he made himself nothing
by taking the very nature of a servant,
being made in human likeness.
And being found in appearance as a human being,
he humbled himself
by becoming obedient to death –
even death on a cross!

Therefore God exalted him to the highest place
and gave him the name that is above every name,
that at the name of Jesus every knee should bow,
in Heaven and on Earth and under the Earth,
and every tongue acknowledge that Jesus Christ is Lord,
to the glory of God the Father.

tion begins with a description of Jesus as 'in God's form', making a decision not to exploit his divine status for himself but to step humbly into the role of servant and human being. Jesus takes a further step down in submitting himself to death, and yet again no ordinary death but one by crucifixion. Through this ordeal, Jesus demonstrates the kind of humility and self-denial that Paul wants to encourage in the Philippians. Paul goes on to say that God acted to reverse this humiliation by exalting Jesus to a position where one day everyone would acknowledge him as the Lord. The striking fact is that the final words of the hymn are quoted directly from Isaiah 45:23, words which the prophet had used of God himself.

In the 1st century, the word 'lord' or 'Lord' had a wide range of meanings. Consequently, there was a kind of sliding scale across which people's thoughts could move up and down when they heard about Jesus in different contexts.

How on earth did Christians come to put Jesus on the same level as God himself? According to the Philippian hymn, God

---

THE DIFFERENT MEANINGS FOR 'LORD'

- It could be a polite form of address, equivalent to the term 'sir'. A respected Rabbi might be addressed as 'Lord'.
- It was also used for a master of slaves – he owned them and their role in life was at his service. He was their lord.
- It was used for the Roman emperor who was the lord of the Roman world.
- It was used for central figures of worship in Greek and Roman religions.
- Among the Jews, the word 'Lord' was used when reading the Scriptures, rather than uttering God's own name.

himself had exalted Jesus to share his divine power and kingdom. Remember it was the resurrected and exalted Jesus in glory who had met Paul outside of Damascus. That he now shares the Kingdom of God is a natural development from Jesus' own claim when he was on trial before the high priest that they would see him sharing God's sovereignty. Acknowledging Jesus as the resurrected Lord was the key Christian confession of faith made on conversion and baptism. As Paul reminds the Christians in Rome:

> If you confess with your mouth that Jesus is Lord and believe in your heart that God raised him from the dead, you will be saved. For with the heart one believes and is justified, and with the mouth one confesses and is saved.
>
> (Romans 10:8–9)

As if that were not enough there is a further early Christian hymn in Colossians 1:15–20. This hymn describes God's Son the king (v. 13). It says he is the visible revelation of the invisible God, something human beings are supposed to be according tothe creation story in Genesis. But this Son is also active in the creation of everything and continues to keep everything together as Lord of the universe. That Christ is God's agent at the Creation leads Christians to speak of his pre-existence, that is, that somehow he was alive and active within God before being born into this world as a human being. We read something similar in the first chapter of John's Gospel where Jesus is identified with the Word of God. Here in Colossians he is often said to be described in terms of the wisdom of God. It was common Jewish thinking that God had created the world by his Word and through his wisdom. Now Christians had come to see and hear the Word and wisdom embodied in Jesus Christ. The Colossian hymn also depicts him as head of his body, the Church. Here we have an echo of the words spoken by Jesus to Paul on the Damascus road: 'Why do you persecute *me?*' The Church is described as his body, the means by which he expresses himself in the world. Then the awesome claim is made that the fullness of God lives in him. It is claims like these which led the early Christians to worship Jesus as they worshipped God. The last verse of the Colossian hymn tells us that God reconciled all things to himself through Jesus, making peace by the blood of his Cross. So the question of how could the death and Resurrection of Jesus have such a colossal impact on the world is answered in terms of who he is.

It is breathtaking to read these descriptions of Jesus in the letters of Paul, who often points to his divinely given commission to teach and preach the truth of the Christian gospel. Many people who come to know and believe in Jesus, even when they had not seen the risen Christ as Paul had, find their lives transformed. This is not to say that Jewish Christians were not sometimes tempted to return to Judaism and that gentile Christians sometimes publicly renounced their faith when persecuted, as we shall see.

For those who had been Jews before they became Christians, Paul's ways of speaking about Jesus must have been particularly difficult to take on board, not only because of what he says about Christ's death but even more so because of who he says Jesus is. Associating him so closely with the position and activities of God might seem to challenge that fundamental Jewish belief of 'the Lord our God is one Lord', but other New Testament writings show

how their authors agreed with Paul and developed some of his ideas.

HOW THE PASTOR OF THE HEBREWS WROTE ABOUT JESUS

The Book of Hebrews begins like a sermon and ends like a letter. The writer called it a message of encouragement and it makes good sense to suppose that the author was pastor of this group of Jewish Christians but separated from them. He is concerned that they might be tempted to go back to Judaism, possibly because of the threat of persecution. Judaism was a protected religion in the Roman Empire and to rejoin the synagogue would shield them from hostile opponents. They may also have been concerned about how the sins they had committed since their conversion could be forgiven. In Judaism there was the annual Day of Atonement when all the unforgiven sins of the previous year could be wiped out and a fresh start made. So how does the pastor address his people?

Traditional ways of speaking about Jesus

He begins by contrasting God's Word in the past through the Prophets with His Word through his Son in 'these last days' (Hebrews 1:1–2). This draws our attention to a distinctive feature of Jewish thinking about history and how this view has been modified by the coming of Jesus. Jews typically think of history in terms of two ages, the present age, and the age to come. At the end of the present age, God will intervene to put right everything that is wrong in the world and bring in the new age, the time when everything will be as it should be. You may remember that in the Gospels Jesus spoke of the future coming of the kingdom of God. Jews expect that when the new age comes, then the kingdom of God will be here. But Jesus also exercises the sovereign power of God. This led to the Christian modification of the Jewish view. For Christians, the Kingdom of God arrives in the figure of Jesus, and some of the gifts of the age to come have already arrived, for example the gift of God's Spirit. But they still pray for God's kingdom to come fully, for the days when people everywhere will be obedient to God's will. So they see themselves living in the decisive last days of the old era. And in these last days God has spoken decisively and authoritatively through his Son. Already there is a hint that to go back to Judaism would be to go back in history.

Then the writer of Hebrews speaks about Jesus in terms reminiscent of Paul. He says the Son is 'the heir of all things' just as he was the one through whom the world had been created. He says that God is seen very clearly revealed in his Son. This is what he means when he says that the Son is 'the radiance', the outshining, 'of the glory of God and the exact imprint of his nature'. The Son keeps everything going. Jesus' death was followed by exaltation to the executive position at God's right hand. The reason why the writer begins with these huge claims is that he wants to encourage the Jewish Christians to remain obedient to the teachings of Jesus which are even more important than the Jewish Law. He sees them in danger of drifting away like a ship which has slipped its moorings.

A *new idea*

The writer of Hebrews then develops an idea which is not in Paul. He stresses the humanity of Jesus as his qualification for the role of high priest. Priests were officials who served in the temple and offered the required sacrifices. The high priest had the special responsibility of going into the Most Holy Place, the innermost shrine of the temple, on the Day of Atonement once a year. And here the writer makes a powerful and extraordinary claim that Jesus is not only the high priest but also the sacrifice. He has entered not the temple in Jerusalem, but Heaven itself, into the very presence of God. In this way, what he has done once is sufficient to deal with all human sins for all times. More than this, Jesus continues to exercise his role as high priest by praying for people in God's very presence. In these ways, the writer claims, Jesus has by his death established the new covenant which the prophet Jeremiah had foretold, a covenant based on forgiveness. The word 'covenant' is one of the most important words in the Bible about the relationship between God and his people. It speaks of a bond, likened in the prophets to the marriage vow. Its basis was the promise made at Mount Sinai where God promised to be God to the people, and they promised to be his people and do everything he told them to do. As they had not lived up to that, so Jeremiah spoke of the coming day when God would make a new covenant. Jesus and writers in the New Testament see the death of Jesus as bringing that new covenant into operation. So, if his readers give up their Christian faith and go back to Judaism, they will lose all the blessings that Christ and his death and Resurrection have brought. He urges them to fix their eyes on Jesus and not jeopardize their spiritual welfare in eternity.

So here in Hebrews we see the gospel about Jesus painted in pictures that are taken from the Jewish and Old Testament Scriptures but are compatible with the portrait drawn by Paul. It appeals to a specific audience, probably in a particular situation, but it also displays who Jesus is and the significance of his work in ways which extend the imagination in different directions from those of Paul.

SUMMARY

- It is clear that the first Christians very early in Christian history came to speak of Jesus as more than an ordinary human being. They thought of him in the highest possible terms and called on him as their Lord in prayer and worship.

- That he had been a remarkable man was clear from the Gospels but, naturally, it was difficult for the disciples to see that he was any more than that until the day of Resurrection, which broke the mould.

- This was followed by his Ascension and the visions of Stephen and Paul who saw him in glory.

- To Jewish outsiders, Christians began with Jesus, the man, and the miracles, but then interpreted his death in terms of God's plan, followed by God's actions in promoting him to glory.

- To both Jews and gentiles, they warned that the Christ would be the final judge but added that forgiveness was possible for those who believed and were baptized, transferring their lives to his ownership.

- To insiders, they elaborated the idea that the death of Christ was part of God's plan and action and developed their understanding that Jesus now shared not only divine nature but divine honours and executive authority. Somehow they saw him having a role in Creation as well as salvation; that he ruled the universe and the Church.

Just how Jesus could be both a human being and share God's role was yet to be worked out and what relation life after Resurrection had to this life would be endlessly debated. But what was so evident by the end of the 1st century, even to the Roman authorities, was that Jesus Christ had grabbed the hearts and minds and lives of many, many people.

Chapter 4

Jesus and the emergence of Christianity

Christianity emerged as a separate religion through a rich, multi-faceted story. By the 5th century, it was not only the established religion of the Roman Empire but a number of Church councils had attempted to define the official version of the Christian faith, including how Christians should think of Jesus. From our reading of the New Testament it is already obvious that people spoke of Jesus within a particular world view which is unusual to many in the 21st century. This world view included the real existence of God who had created the world by his Word. He was involved throughout human history but in some sense he had come into the world through Jesus, his Son. The purpose of the life, death and Resurrection of Jesus was nothing less than the remaking of people and the world. If we are to appreciate what Jesus meant in this context, we need to use our imaginations and step into this world view.

In the early centuries CE, Christianity separated from Judaism so that it became a different religion, at least as far as Jews were concerned. At the same time across the Roman world different groups of Christians promoted sometimes radically different versions of their faith. This all took place in situations which were often dangerous and where many were called upon to testify to their faith as martyrs. A revolution in imperial policy in the fourth century made Christianity the official religion of the Roman Empire, but this did not end persecution for those who found themselves out of favour with the powerful. One of the major causes of the troubles during the 4th and 5th centuries was the crucial issue of how to speak when speaking about Jesus. Words carried meaning and the wrong words could undermine people's faith and hope. Pictures carry meaning, too, and we can see how Christians thought of Jesus from the ways in which they portrayed him visually.

CHRISTIANS AND JEWS DRIFT APART
Why they separated

Christians regarded themselves as the people of God, a new development in the history of Israel it is true, but nevertheless one in which the promises of God in the Scriptures were fulfilled. They took over the Greek translation of the Hebrew Scriptures as their Bible and interpreted their faith by its stories and prophecies. This is not to say that all Christians thought that they had replaced the Jews as God's people. Paul had warned gentile believers that their inclusion did not mean the exclusion of those to whom God first made the promises. Yet his language had sufficient ambiguity to allow people to miss his point. There were tensions between Jews and Christians in New Testament times and in the years that followed, the parting of the ways between the synagogue and the Church became clearer to all.

　　This separation cannot be precisely dated. The continued

presence of Jewish Christian communities tended to blur the distinctions. But most Christians proclaimed a message which many Jews could not accept. Jews did not see Jesus as their Messiah for the world seemed to go on pretty much the same after Jesus as it had before. If anything, instead of the fulfilment of the great prophecies of peace and prosperity, matters had gotten worse. In 70 CE the temple itself was destroyed and the city of Jerusalem sacked. The Jewish Christian community had escaped from the city before the final Roman assault but Palestinian Jewry had been decimated. All that remained in Judea was the rabbinic school at Jamnia established by Pharisees with Roman permission. This was to be the centre of rabbinic Judaism but it was hardly what they expected would happen when the Messiah came.

Another key issue which divided Jews from Christians was the way the latter would talk about the deity of Christ and give him honour and worship. The Book of Revelations in the New Testament includes a clear picture of heavenly worship directed both to God and to the Messiah. This, for Jews, threatened their belief that God was one and that worship should be directed to him alone. The rabbis talked about a heretical group 'who say there are two powers in Heaven' and concluded that these heretics were ditheists, that is, believers in two gods. This may well have been directed at Christians.

A major factor in the separation of Christians and Jews was the second Jewish revolt against the Romans [132–135 CE]. The leader, Simeon bar Kosiba, called himself 'Prince of Israel' and was hailed as bar Kokhba, that is, 'Son of the Star'. This was a reference to a prophecy in the biblical Book of Numbers which said 'a star shall come out of Jacob and a sceptre shall rise out of Israel'.

This text was widely understood to predict the coming of a conquering Messiah who would defeat Rome and set Israel free. In fact Simeon was proclaimed Messiah by the famous Rabbi Akiba [50–132 CE]. Here was a clear challenge to Christian claims about Jesus and at first one more likely to be accepted by Jews. But the revolt was savagely crushed, the Jewish state destroyed and Jews were banned from Jerusalem. Christians moved away from stressing the Jewish roots of their faith to defending it in terms of Greek philosophy.

A 2ⁿᵈ century discussion

In Justin Martyr's *Dialogue with Trypho* [156 CE], we hear a Christian and a Jew discussing points of difference between them. The historical setting is towards the end of the war which followed bar Kokhba's rebellion. Trypho and Justin meet casually, probably in Ephesus, and Trypho introduces himself as a refugee from the war. He agrees that all the Jews are expecting the Messiah and that the Scriptures speak of him. He says he is impressed by the name Jesus ('Joshua' in the Hebrew Scriptures) for that name means 'Saviour'. But, he continues, 'we doubt if the Christ could have been crucified in this dishonourable way for he who is crucified is said by the law to be cursed, so on that point I am most unwilling to be convinced'. He is prepared to accept that the Scriptures spoke of a suffering Messiah but not of one suffering the curse of the Law. This is the same issue which we saw troubling Paul before his conversion. Justin replies that Christians believe in the same God as the Jews but that through Christ's suffering on the Cross, God has established a new and better covenant. For Justin the Scriptures speak directly about Christ. In fact Justin believes that Jesus himself was speaking in the Scriptures before he came into the world and he predicted what would happen. On this basis Justin argues that Jesus foretold his own Crucifixion, Resurrection and Ascension, and he produces what he thinks are appropriate references. In particular he draws Trypho's attention to Isaiah 53 which speaks of someone being led to execution, dishonoured, beaten and killed like sheep led to slaughter. Justin says that anyone who hears this chapter read will think it describes a man being crucified. He tries to back this up by using other scriptures in support.

Trypho also raises the question of the divinity of Jesus. He asks if the Christian claim that Christ is divine does not mean there is 'another God in addition to the Creator of the world'. Justin refers him to the story in Genesis 18 where three men visit Abraham. Two of these men turn out to be angels who rescue Lot from Sodom in the next chapter. The third is called 'the Lord' and Justin argues that he is someone different from the Creator, but not a rival, for he only does and says what God intended. When asked to prove that this was Jesus, Justin appeals to the idea of 'a rational power' or word [Gk. *logos*]. Just as a person's thoughts or words are not separate from that person so the *logos* of God was not separate from God. He was with God at the Creation and his presence explains the plural reference in the story of Creation when God says, 'Let us make man in our own image'. This is the Word which became a human being in Jesus Christ as the opening verses of John's Gospel show, he says.

Trypho partially agrees with this line of argument but he now asks how this God who was seen by Abraham came to be born of a virgin as a real human being. He knows that Christians appeal to Isaiah 7:14, a verse which is quoted in Matthew chapter 1. This reads in Matthew as: 'Behold a virgin shall conceive and bear a son'. Trypho points out that the word in Isaiah means a 'young woman' not a 'virgin', and says her son will be King Hezekiah. He then criticizes Justin for telling legends about Jesus which are like the Greek myths of Zeus. Instead Justin should say Jesus had a normal human birth. Justin responds by arguing that the Greek legends were in fact distorted versions of prophecies which speak of Christ, and for the translation of Isaiah 7:14, he appeals to the Greek Bible which has the same word ('virgin') found in Matthew's Gospel.

Here we have an erudite discussion based on common scriptures which are understood differently. The discussion is conducted in friendly terms and concludes with both sides expressing their enjoyment. 'We should do this more often,' they say. There are weak links in Justin's case but, taken as a whole, it demonstrates how much searching of the Scriptures Christians had done to try to establish their faith for themselves, and to commend it to others. It also illustrates the Christian belief that Jesus was the turning point of human history. He was not only the climax of Israel's history but he fulfilled the distorted hopes of pagan writers, too. The use of the word *logos* for Jesus was an excellent bridge between Jewish and Greek worlds, as we shall see.

A call for complete separation

About 150 CE Marcion (see pp. 19–20) argued that Christianity was a completely separate faith from Judaism. He taught that the father of Jesus was not the God of the Old Testament who had created the world because that God frequently ordered actions which were contrary to the teachings of Jesus. For example, he ordered the slaughter of the Canaanites, while Jesus taught people to love their enemies. Instead, the father of Jesus was the unknown God that Paul had spoken about to the people of Athens. So there were two gods, as the Jews feared. The Messiah foretold in the Hebrew Bible was for the Jews and would restore their kingdom. He was not for Christians. Jesus, on the other hand, represented the grace of God in contrast to the justice of the Law. Marcion denied the reality of the virgin birth and argued that Jesus only appeared to have a human body and to suffer. This radical solution went too far for many Christians and the Church in Rome expelled him. He went off and founded churches elsewhere and his churches flourished particularly in Syria. They were not the only variation among Christian communities.

CHRISTIAN DIVERSITY

Evidence for different views of Jesus can be found in the many writings which survive from the 2nd century onwards. Some of these attacked heretics and their books. These 'heretics' were groups who followed particular individual teachers and separated themselves from other Christians. Celsus, an able opponent of Christians, distinguished the 'Great Church' from numerous sects. Among these sects were Jewish Christian groups and others loosely classified today as Gnostics, while the 'Great Church' comprised those who were effectively the seeds of an emerging orthodoxy. The idea of an 'emerging orthodoxy' might be thought premature at this stage but in fact there were those who spoke of Jesus in ways shaped by apostolic traditions, both oral and written. The four Gospels – Matthew, Mark, Luke and John – together with the letters of Paul, were already widely quoted as authoritative sources for what should be said about Jesus. These writings were also regularly read out in meetings for Christian worship and used for teaching and preaching so they were widely known.

Supplementing the Gospels

Not all the popular writings of the second century were for or against heretics. Some were written to satisfy curiosity about what had happened to Jesus at times where the four Gospels tell us nothing. What happened, for example, between his birth and when he went up to the temple at the age of twelve? The so-called Infancy Gospels supply some of the missing details. In the *Infancy Gospel of Thomas* we read about Jesus at the age of five. One day, he was playing by a stream. He made twelve sparrows of clay. This was reported to Joseph who rebuked him, because it was a Sabbath, but Jesus clapped his hands and the sparrows flew away. Even as a child, Jesus called back to life another boy who had fallen from the roof of his house and healed another who had injured his foot while chopping wood. On another occasion, he miraculously lengthened a piece of wood for Joseph. At the same time a child who ran into Jesus dropped dead on the spot, and when the parents complained, he struck them with blindness. He was a precocious child and no rabbis could teach him anything. These stories are significant because, on the one hand, they satisfied questions often asked by the faithful but, on the other, they illustrate what was spurious when compared with the 1st century Gospels.

The Gnostics

Among the churches dotted all over the Roman Empire were some whose leaders are today called gnostics. One of their most famous texts is the *Gospel of Thomas* found at Nag Hammadi in Egypt in 1945, but already partly known in Greek in *The Sayings of Jesus*, published in 1897 and 1904.

GNOSTICISM

Gnosticism was a climate of ideas, a world view which saw the physical world as evil and in darkness; only a higher spiritual realm of light was good. God was spiritual and far too remote to have any direct contact with people or with this material world. He was not even its creator. Rather there were many spiritual forces which occupied the space between this world and the world above. One of these forces had been responsible for creation. This relieved God of responsibility for evil. Human beings were made up of body (evil) and soul/spirit (good). Fragments of light from the higher realm had become trapped in their bodies so they had an inner light but they were enslaved by powerful cosmic forces like fate. These were sometimes referred to as 'the rulers of this world'. The human quest was for freedom from this world to regain the realm of light and truth. Christ was one of many spiritual forces between this world and the world above. Jesus had been a spiritual revelation of the Christ rather than an incarnation of God. He came from the world of light to reveal the light. This light was the secret knowledge or insight (*gnosis*) through which people could be saved by becoming aware of their own true selves. They could then be reunited with the realm of light. Gnostics took their stand on verses like John 8:32: 'you will know the truth and the truth will set you free'. In fact it was one of the gnostics, Heracleon, who wrote the first commentary on John's Gospel. It is interesting that some people today follow 'new-age' ideas which often seem to echo these 2nd century gnostics.

It begins with 'the secret sayings which the living Jesus spoke.' It goes on to promise immortal life to those who find the true meaning of the sayings. The secret or mystery here is not like the mystery of the kingdom of God in the New Testament Gospels. That is about God's plan of salvation which is clearly revealed to all. The mystery here is for one group only and distinguishes them from the rest. The sayings present Jesus as a teacher of wisdom and deny that any of the Jewish Scriptures are related to him. Jesus' teaching about the future of the kingdom has disappeared. Instead we read about the kingdom as an inner, spiritual and time-less reality. This gospel sometimes corrects the teaching of Jesus in the New Testament Gospels. For example one saying recalls Jesus' question to the disciples about what people were saying about him. In the synoptic gospels, the disciples replied, 'one of the prophets'. Here the disciples reply, 'a righteous angel', 'a wise philosopher'. Thomas, rather than Peter, plays the leading role. He says that he cannot find words to describe Jesus and Jesus takes him apart from the others to give him secret teaching. This explains why the *Gospel of Thomas* points to a mysterious under-standing of Jesus which even other the disciples do not have.

The principal concern of the *Gospel of Thomas* is to foster a spirituality in which individuals discover their heavenly origin and find their own true selves. Jesus indicates that he has come from Heaven and says that others can share in this divine 'equality'. Saying 28 recalls the classic gnostic saviour myth which tells how the saviour enters the world to find humanity drunk, blind and sleeping. His role is to wake some of them up and bring them to true knowledge of themselves and their salvation. What Jesus says is more important than who he is. He simply declares these secret sayings, offering to the few, spiritual insight which is not available to others.

Inevitably gnostics rejected the idea that Jesus rose physically from the dead. Rather, Resurrection was a symbol of the continuing presence of Christ with believers. What mattered was not seeing him alive literally but spiritual vision. The *Gospel of Mary* explains spiritual visions in terms of dreams or trances. When Mary Magdalene saw the Lord in a vision she asked 'How does he who sees the vision see it? (Through) the soul, (or) through the spirit?' Christ answered, 'through the mind'. In the *Apocalypse of Peter* Christ tells Peter, 'I am the intellectual spirit, filled with radiant light.' This fits the sketch of gnosticism given above but it teaches a very different gospel from the New Testament. At the same time these writings stress the reality of these visions. With shades of Indian teachers they claim the world is unreal and Resurrection is a moment of present spiritual enlightenment.

It is not surprising that these writers set little store by the death of Christ. The *Apocalypse of Peter* gives an account which is very different from that in the New Testament. Peter says:

> I saw him apparently being seized by them. And I said, 'What am I seeing, O Lord? Is it really you whom they take? And are you holding on to me? And are they hammering the feet and hands of another? Who is this one above the Cross, who is glad and laughing?' The Saviour said to me, 'He whom you saw being glad and laughing above the Cross is the living Jesus. But he into whose hands and feet they are driving the nails is his fleshly part, which is the substitute. They put to shame that which remained in his likeness. And look at him, and [look] at me!'

Here we have a distinction between one who appears to be
Jesus, his material body which can be crucified, and 'the living
Jesus' above the Cross. Peter learns that only the body dies, the
spirit is set free to be united with 'the perfect light'. In another
text it is explained that Simon who carried the Cross for Jesus was
crucified and that Jesus was laughing at their ignorance. Humanly
speaking, these may be the sources for later Muslim ideas.

Defenders of the faith

Teaching like this prompted others to respond that it undermined the basic pillars of the faith. Such writers based their
views on the writings of the Apostles which survived from the
1st century. From them came claims about the divinity of Christ
and the humanity of Jesus. Very early in the 2nd century Ignatius
of Antioch wrote to the Church at Ephesus of the one physician
both human and divine, from Mary and from God. He was 'really
born and ate and drank, really persecuted by Pontius Pilate, really
crucified and died . . . really rose from the dead' to destroy
death and bring new life. Only God could accomplish salvation,
but only through his being a real human could he rescue other
human beings.

Towards the end of the 2nd century Irenaeus, Bishop of Lyons,
defended the faith against the gnostics in his five books *Against
the Heresies*. His basic point was that the Christian faith was
'spoken with one voice', by which he meant agreed in churches
throughout the Roman world. This was clearly an exaggeration
but Irenaeus added that this faith was based on the tradition,
that is, the teaching handed down from the Apostles. This tradition was not secret but available to all in the holy writings. He

taught that Jesus was born of the Virgin, taking a real body. He resisted temptation by the Devil and overcame death on the Cross. Christ had retraced the story of Adam and the human race and by his obedience, in place of Adam's disobedience, made salvation possible for all. He had passed through all the stages of life, infant, child, youth and adult that he might bring all to share his divine life. He became what we are in order to make us what he is. All that was lost in Adam is won back by Christ. He really died and rose, going bodily into Heaven. He is the Christians' Lord. He will come again to restore all things and raise the dead so that all will acknowledge him as Lord and King. Irenaeus explained the relationship between the Father, the Son and the Spirit by saying the Son and the Spirit, as Word and Wisdom, were the two hands of the one God. This gospel, said Irenaeus, was the Rule of Faith and a means of distinguishing truth from heresy.

He accused the gnostics of passing off what they themselves had written as apostolic. 'For what they have published . . . is totally unlike what has been handed down to us from the Apostles.' He criticized them for calling their own feelings, ideas and experiences divine revelation. Against these he set the four Gospels written by Jesus' disciples and their followers, and he said that the Apostles 'like a rich man depositing money in a bank, placed in the Church fully everything that belongs to truth: so that everyone, whoever will, can draw from her the water of life'. He attacked gnostic devaluation of the body because it justified their claim that Christ suffered only in his human nature, not his divine nature. Such a belief divided Christ into two natures. But in reality he was both and suffered as both.

The Alexandrians

One city stands out as the centre of many of the debates and some-times violent disagreements about the nature of Jesus. That city was Alexandria, at that time the capital of Egypt and a famous centre of learning. Its library was said to contain 700,000 volumes and it was home to poets, mathematicians, geographers, doctors, chemists, astronomers and philosophers. It also became the city of a famous theological school and teachers at this school commended the Christian faith to educated inquirers. One of these was Clement [150–215 CE]. He used ideas similar to those of some of the gnostics, although he criticized them at the same time. He argued that Greek philosophy was a preparation for the gospel for gentiles as the Law had been for Jews. He exploited the different meanings of the word *logos* to speak of Jesus. The word *logos* for the Greeks explained the rationality and order of the cosmos. It explained why there was a world and why it was a cosmos – some-thing of order and beauty – and not a chaos. But *logos* also means reason and rationality in human beings and is often translated 'word'. People use words to express themselves. In the Bible the Word was the dynamic, creative power of God and his means of speaking to people. Now Clement could say, this *logos* was embodied in Jesus. This was a way of referring to his divine nature. He was both God and man 'becoming man in order that such as you may learn from man how it is even possible for man to become a god'.

Another influential Alexandrian was Origen [185–254 CE]. He taught that the incarnation was necessary to reverse the fall of humankind. By identifying with Jesus, Christians can be restored to God. Christ's real humanity was the means of bringing God and human beings together. Jesus had suffered death to release people from the power of death 'for no one who is with Jesus can be seized by death'. But Origen sowed the seeds of future debates by stressing that the Son was subordinate to the Father because he derived his being from the Father. That is what a Father–Son relationship means. At the same time he said both the Father and the Son lived eternally in that relationship.

You can tell this was in a university setting, can't you! But it is important to see what was at stake here. The one, real, living God became a human being in Jesus. Only God could save people so God himself had come into the human situation to rescue human beings. But this raised questions. How then were God and Jesus related? Had God really suffered and died on the Cross? Was Jesus truly someone who shared our humanity so that he could sympathize with and comfort those going through fiery trials? There were many believers who suffered the ultimate penalty for their faith in Jesus Christ. How did their understanding of martyrdom affect their understanding of Jesus?

PERSECUTION

Persecution, including death for the faith, went back to New Testament days. Such evidence as we have also implies that Peter and Paul met their deaths in Rome shortly after the fire of 64 CE. But historians tend to draw a big picture and say persecution was local and sporadic before the reign of the Emperor Decius [249–251 CE]. This is not to say that being a victim of a local persecution was any less traumatic than dying in a general one. Christians were savaged in the arena by wild animals or, if they were Roman citizens like Justin, beheaded. Some were starved to death, others burned alive. Governors often offered them a way out. They had only to offer incense and wine to the emperor's statue and recite a prayer to the Roman gods and curse Christ. These were simple loyalty tests but totally impossible for those who died to comply. Their deaths show what they thought of Jesus and the strength of their commitment to him as their Lord. He was King of kings and therefore loyalty to him prevented them 'worshipping' the emperor.

This was where the reality of Christ's own suffering was a vital support to martyrs. Hippolytus, who witnessed the persecution ordered by Emperor Severus in 202 CE, wrote:

> If he were not of the same nature with ourselves, he would command in vain that we should imitate the teacher . . . He did not protest against his Passion, but became obedient unto death . . . now in all these acts he offered up, as the first fruits, his own humanity, in order that you, when you are in tribulation, may not be discouraged, but, confessing yourself to be one like the redeemer, may dwell in expectation of receiving what the Father has granted the Son.
>
> (Hippolytus, *Refutation of All Heresies*, 10.33)

Sometimes other Christians saw Jesus himself present in the victim. So, for example, in 177 CE at Lyons, a slave girl called Blandina was suspended upside down from a post in the arena and Christians who watched commented that 'she seemed to hang there in the form of a Cross and by her fervent prayer she aroused intense enthusiasm in those who were undergoing their ordeal for they saw in their struggle and with their physical sight, him who was crucified on their behalf in the person of their sister Blandina' (*The Acts of Christian Martyrs*, ed. H. Mursurillo, Oxford: Clarendon 1972 p. 41).

Persecution as imperial policy

In 249 CE Decius, who had been a very successful general defeating the barbarians in Europe, was acclaimed emperor by his troops. He was the one who initiated the first empire-wide persecution of Christians. They were regarded as a threat to the security of the empire as they undermined loyalty to the emperor and the gods from within. Their claim that Jesus was the King of kings made their loyalty to him take priority over their loyalty to the emperor. This the emperor could not tolerate. Bishops were executed or went into hiding. Christians were lynched, dragged to temples and forced to sacrifice to the gods. They had their homes and properties looted and destroyed. An edict was published in 250 CE that everyone must sacrifice to the gods and get a certificate to prove that they had done so. It was significant that this persecution was carried out by Roman officials with little or no support from the ordinary citizen, many of whom came to the assistance of their Christian neighbours. Further edicts against Christians followed from time to time throughout the remaining years of the 3rd century although they were interspersed with more favourable times. Persecution came to a head again under Emperor Diocletian [284–305], despite the fact that his wife and daughter were Christians. In 303 CE church buildings and Bibles were destroyed, clergy were arrested and the edict compelling sacrifice to the gods was renewed.

Imperial policy reversed

The revolution came with Emperor Constantine, from 312 to 337. He defeated Maxentius, the last of six rival emperors, at the Battle of Milvian Bridge, north of Rome, in 313 CE and so brought a period of civil war to an end. According to the early church historian Eusebius, Constantine had seen a vision of the Cross in the sky and in a dream the night before the battle he was told to mark his soldiers' shields with the badge of Christ, a monogram made up of the first two Greek letters of Christ's name *chi* with *rho* super-imposed on it. He concluded that his victory was due to the God of the Christians. He now issued an edict tolerating all religious cults and restoring all Christian property. This meant that Christians were no longer the enemies of the state. While the toleration part of the edict did not last long and the emperor's behaviour was not what everyone would call Christian, persecution was no longer directed at the 'Great Church'. In 380 CE Christianity became the official religion of the empire. But this did not mean that all Christians were now agreed about how to speak of Jesus.

DRAWING THE BOUNDARIES OF ORTHODOXY

As we have seen, the key questions about Jesus which occupied some of the finest minds from the 2nd to the 5th centuries were questions about how to speak of Jesus in relation to God. If God was one how could people attribute divinity to Jesus without speaking of two gods? And could God suffer? Most of the partici-pants in these debates seemed to think that God could not suffer, an idea which seems to have come from Greek philosophy and is different from the biblical story of God. But if Jesus were not God how could Christians worship him and how could he save the world? If Jesus had been a real human being, how could he be said to share God's nature? If, on the other hand, it was insisted that he was somehow God, how could he have been a real man? How were his human and divine natures related? And all this was discussed in the context of what has been called 'the most profound of all the mysteries of being', the Trinity.

This might all sound rather abstract and esoteric to readers today. It is hard to recapture the atmosphere in Constantinople according to Bishop Gregory of Nyssa in the early 380s. He said everyone in the streets of the city was talking about these questions. If you asked someone for some change, inquired about the price of a loaf, or asked whether your bath was ready, you would get some comment about how God the Father was related to the Son in reply. These questions really mattered to these people. They accepted the reality of God and that somehow God had come into the world in Jesus. Yet Jesus was a real human being who had fully shared human experience that he might reconcile people to God.

One method of addressing these questions was to hit on helpful analogies. For example the sun and its rays were one light and yet that one could be spoken of in the plural, the rays. In the same way a spring and its tributaries were one and several. Tertullian spoke of a plant which has a root, a shoot and fruit. Augustine suggested that the relationship between memory, understanding and will in the human mind, or between mind, knowledge and love in human beings provided possible ways of thinking about God who had revealed himself as three and one. He acknowledged the inadequacy of human words to speak about God but said these one-in-three aspects of the human mind were 'footprints of the Trinity'. Pictures might be suggestive ways of illustrating what people already believed but were not compelling to those not yet persuaded.

Controversies

Shortly after Constantine's adoption of Christianity controversy broke out in Alexandria. An elder named Arius [250–336] objected to his bishop's teaching that God the Father and God the Son were one and the same. For Arius this obscured an essential distinction. God himself was unknowable and unreachable. He alone was eternal and had no beginning. It had become accepted to speak of Jesus as 'the only begotten of the Father' to show that he shared the same nature as God – like begets like. But Arius pointed out that if he was begotten, there must have been a time before that, when he did not exist. Arius logically underlined the subordination of the Son to the Father. He also claimed that in Jesus, the Word had taken the place of the soul/spirit in a normal human being. This implied that Jesus was less than God and more than a human being. He was neither God nor man. If this were true it could no longer be claimed that God was revealed in Christ or that what he had done to save people actually reached them. The Church was split, some calling for Arius to be disciplined and others supporting him. He was excommunicated and eventually exiled. The arguments which followed were often violent and the conflict political, involving exile, bloodshed, armies and police. To understand this we must remember what was at stake.

Constantine was not preoccupied with resolving these 'very small and insignificant questions', but was concerned about the unity of the Church. A council of over 200 bishops was called at Nicaea in 325 CE. This was the first of the ecumenical councils although the overwhelming majority were from the eastern part of the empire. The emperor himself presided. He expressed the hope that his military victories over tyrants would now be followed by peace in the Church of God. It was a vain hope. Arius was condemned and the council agreed, with two abstentions, that the Son shared the same being or essence with the Father. The essence of Jesus was the essence of God. This established that God was knowable through and active in Jesus and that as the Son, Jesus shared God's eternal nature; he had not been created. But it did not end the controversy which continued largely because the Greek word used to express the idea that the Son shared the same being as the Father was not found in the Bible, and because it had been used by heretics to obscure the difference between the Father and the Son.

One champion of the Nicaea formula, who found himself virtually isolated among the eastern bishops, was Athanasius, Bishop of Alexandria [296–373]. He was one of the most trenchant critics of Arian views. He showed from the Scriptures that Jesus was both divine and human, not separately, but together. 'It was the Word who performed miracles and who wept, was hungry, prayed, and cried out from the Cross.' Only one who fully shares the reality of the Father could save people from ignorance, corruptibility and death. Only one who is not a created being could not be captured by death. But he destroyed death and corruption in a mortal body so that humanity might be renewed in the image of God. God stooped down to humanity in his Son to raise humanity to God through the incarnation of the Word whose death 'effects humanity's deification'. Only such a Jesus could bring human beings to share the life of God himself. Eventually, after much not very edifying political power play with bishops being exiled and restored, the Council of Constantinople

[381 CE] agreed the Nicaean formula, added a clause about the Holy Spirit and declared the three persons were equally one God. Athanasius had triumphed but not lived to see the victory.

There was still an unsettled question about how the divine and human natures of Jesus were related to each other. Nestorius [d. 451], Bishop of Constantinople, argued the two natures in Christ were separate and not mixed up together. He said he could not give the name God to a two- or three-month-old baby. He also attacked the idea that Mary was 'the mother of God'. She was the mother of the man Jesus, he said. His followers understood his reference to two natures to mean two persons and they appealed to the titles Son of God and Son of Man in the Gospels to substantiate their claim. This view was condemned at the Council of Ephesus [431] and the Council of Chalcedon [451]. The Definition of Faith of the Council of Chalcedon has remained the classic Christian definition of the person of Christ as one person in two natures. It made four positive statements in opposition to four heresies: the true deity of Christ [against the Arians], the full humanity of Christ, the unity of Christ [against the Nestorians], and that the divine and human natures of Christ were not confused. This was a statement of faith which attempted to rule out some ways in which Christian belief about Jesus Christ was expressed. Predictably it did not end the debates which continue today.

HOW WAS JESUS SEEN?

From the 3rd century onwards, we have physical evidence of ways in which Christians saw their faith. This evidence is in wall paintings, buildings, sculptures, and mosaics. These are found in Christian meeting houses, catacombs, villas and so on. Christians had been hesitant about portraying Jesus because, like the Jews, they understood the second of the ten commandments to prohibit the making of any representation of God. But this reluctance seems to have been overcome to provide aids to devotion and ways of recalling stories or titles of Jesus. Some converts replaced their household gods with statues of Jesus. One of the most frequent representations is a shepherd carrying a sheep. This is said to be a pre-Christian symbol for gentleness and kindness but one taken over by Christians who remembered the teaching of Jesus that he was the Good Shepherd. It is easy to see how this would comfort Christians who met in the catacombs to remember those who had died. They would have read or recited Psalm 23 ('The Lord is my shepherd') with its assurance of his presence with them in death, as words about Jesus. One of the most splendid pictures of Jesus as the Good Shepherd is the late 5th century mosaic at Ravenna. From the early 5th century in the north of Italy, a panel of a binding for a copy of the Gospels has among other figures a lamb in the wreath of victory over death. This recalls ideas about the risen Jesus in the Book of Revelations as the victorious slain lamb, and also perhaps the ideas of sacrifice and victory combined in Christ's death.

A sign which marked out Jesus in some of these pictures was a halo. This kind of ring of light or disk had been used by pagan artists to distinguish the most important characters in their pictures. There is evidence of its use not only by Greeks and Romans but further east among Hindus and Buddhists. In Christian pictures when a lamb was used to represent Christ the Lamb of God it was sometimes given a halo. It was only during the 5th century that the halo began to be given to other characters.

Early Christians also found comfort in the Old Testament stories of God saving people in dire situations. Noah, Jonah, Daniel, Daniel's three friends and Ezekiel's vision of the valley of dry bones are among the pictures. On the basis of their faith in the Resurrection of Christ these stories would have given them hope in times of persecution and death. The other favourite picture of Jesus, from the late 3rd century on, is of a teacher instructing his disciples. He is depicted in a typical philosopher's robe, sometimes with a scroll or an open book in one hand with the other hand raised to emphasize the points he is making.

An interesting picture of Christ as a beardless youth, burnt in gold on glass, can be seen in the British Museum. It is sometimes suggested that a youth symbolized divinity or immortality, an encouragement for Christians in a hostile world. Various other symbols pointing to Christ are found at different sites. The sign of the fish with the Greek word for 'fish' enclosed within it would have reminded them of 'Jesus Christ, Son of God, Saviour' because the Greek letters for the word 'fish' are also the first letters of each of these words. It was a neat way of summing up some of the names for Jesus. A drawing in the catacomb of St Domitilla, just outside Rome (early 4th century), shows a fish combined with an anchor in the shape of a cross expressing hope. Another sign frequently found is the *chi-rho* monogram. A monogram is two or more letters interwoven in the form of a badge or sign. One has been reconstructed from fragments found at a Roman villa at Lullingstone in Kent. The *chi* which is the first letter of 'Christ' in Greek is combined with *alpha* and *omega* meaning the beginning and the end. This recalls the Christian beliefs that Jesus is the Messiah and that all of creation came into being through him and everything will be summed up in him at the end of time. The guidebook to the site at Lullingstone says this badge was painted on the south wall of the antechamber to the room used by the house church.

There were significant changes in Christian pictography after the conversion of Constantine. Christ is now portrayed in majesty with the *alpha* and *omega* on either side, as in the 4th century catacomb of Commodilla to the south of Rome. Another 4th century sarcophagus in Rome shows Christ reigning over the universe. Christ sits enthroned, between two elaborately carved scrolls, higher than the figures on either side. In his left hand, he holds a scroll and his right hand is raised in blessing. Beneath his feet the cosmos is personified. It proclaims his victory over death. In another 4th century sculpture the Cross is blended into Constantine's victory standard with the crown of thorns replaced by a laurel wreath of victory. Earlier pictures concentrated on stories from his life and ideas of salvation, such as Jesus calling Lazarus back from the grave. After Constantine, Jesus is presented as a powerful figure and the light of the world. There is a striking mosaic of Christ as the Sungod with a vine in the background in the vaulting of a burial chamber under St Peter's in Rome. It may have encouraged the families of those who were buried there to recall Jesus' words that he is the light of the world. Mosaics elsewhere on floors and walls incorporate many different animals, fish and birds, taking over motifs from Roman art. For example an early 4th century mosaic at Hinton St Mary, in Dorset, shows Christ with pomegranates and the Tree of Life, both of which point to eternal life. The defeat of death and evil is presented in the classical figures of Bellerophon slaying the Chimera. This all suggests that Christianity had now arrived as the religion of the (Roman) world and readily uses classical motifs to express a Christian message.

Chapter 5

Jesus in an age of devotion

In the middle of the 15th century, one of the most far-reaching technical inventions of all time began to transform human life and culture. In the city of Mainz, in the Rhineland, Johann Gutenberg invented a machine for printing using moveable type. The first dated work from his press is a Latin psalter of the year 1454. From then on, instead of copying books by hand, thousands of identical copies could be produced at one printing. At about the same time the capital of the Roman Empire in the east, Constantinople, fell into Muslim hands and Justinian's great church of St Sophia was turned into a mosque. This suggests that the 15th century was a significant turning point in human history. Before then, the period from the 5th or 6th centuries is sometimes called the era of Christian civilization but it was marked by power struggles between emperors and leaders of the Church. There was rivalry between the Bishop of Rome (the pope) and the patriarchs of the eastern church. From the 7th century the eastern churches lost territory to the rise of Islam even if they also expanded further north through missions to the Slavs. European countries responded to the pope's appeal to mount crusades against heretics and to free the holy places in Palestine from Muslim control but the armies were sometimes used against eastern churches.

But the essence of Jesus is not easily found in political and military power struggles. Rather we need to turn to the churches and monasteries, to popular and more esoteric expressions of spirituality. There were clearly two different ways of living the Christian life: what we might call full-time vocational or 'professional' religious life and the popular religion of stories, ceremonies and great occasions. We will find Jesus in pictures, an incredible wealth of paintings, frescoes, reliefs, icons, and illuminated manuscripts. He is also encountered in processions, pilgrimages and miracle plays. People chanted and sang or recited poems about him, or preached in the open air. Finally we can look into the writings of the mystics and the theologians.

JESUS IN PICTURES

Once again we need to recall the significance of the different contexts within which these pictures are, or were, seen. Different contexts prompt different meanings. Today many of these paintings are found in art galleries and museums where they celebrate human achievement but when they were painted, both artists and patrons used them in churches and homes as aids to devotion. Many were altarpieces and painted to be seen in the context of the Eucharist or the Mass, itself one of the most powerful of all picture dramas. When we look at them we see something foreign perhaps, but inviting us to compare life as we know it with what we see. There are some constant features of human nature which allow us to empathize with and to understand people of a bygone world. But we have to recognize that the original context of these pictures was prayer and worship. Clearly, too, we will appreciate this dimension more fully if we visit, for example, the National Gallery or spend some time looking at reproductions in books or exhibition catalogues. Two valuable resources for this purpose are Gabriele Finaldi's *The Image of Christ: The Catalogue of the Exhibition Seeing Salvation*, held in the National Gallery in 2000 CE and the accompanying book, *Seeing Salvation: Images of Christ in Art*, by Neil Macgregor with Erika Langmuir.

The Iconoclastic controversy

But was it right to paint pictures or icons of Jesus? In the 8th and 9th centuries, fierce controversies raged over this question particularly in the Eastern or Orthodox churches, and people went round destroying what they took to be idolatrous images, clearly forbidden in the second of God's Ten Commandments. In any case, if Jesus were divine, how could his divine glory possibly be painted? Was it possible to depict Christ as the God-man? The defenders of icons and pictures replied that the doctrines of creation, and the incar-

---

ICONS

Icons were sometimes said to be an extension of the incarnation or a door into the divine realm, a meeting point between divine grace and human need. The spiritual world was held to manifest itself in and through the material world. So icons were painted in the context of prayer and used in contexts of devotion. In orthodox liturgy, icons embodied the presence of the spiritual world. They helped to meet that human passion which was so characteristic of this age, the passion to get close to God, to know Him, and to share in His divine nature.

nation, invited such representation of God. They distinguished worship that should be given to God alone from honour given to that which represented him or the Virgin, or the saints. John of Damascus in the 8th century saw the Old Testament prohibition of images as a sign of the future coming of God in the flesh and said that after the incarnation such images were allowed. By becoming a man God had made it possible to paint a portrait of that man, and God had created the painters' art and materials. A 15th century Franciscan preacher gave three reasons for religious images in churches: first so that the ignorant and illiterate might learn the faith, second to stir people's natural emotional sluggishness and move them to devotion, and third to act as reminders to people who otherwise would forget what they had heard. Although there were further iconoclastic outbursts at later periods, in general the defenders of icons and pictures won the day.

Medieval art

An example of a picture from the 10th century is the Nativity in the Anglo-Saxon Benedictional of St Aethelwold, now kept in the British Library. It can be viewed with a helpful commentary on the CD *Images of Salvation: The Story of the Bible through Medieval Art* (see Bibliography). This manuscript miniature, which measures approximately 210 x 150 mm, shows the Virgin and a midwife who holds a cushion behind Mary's head and Joseph. The midwife, who is not mentioned in the New Testament but appears in the 2nd century Gospel of James, is indicating to Joseph that the bright cloud signifies the divine nature of the birth. So where is Jesus? In the bottom left-hand corner of the page lying on a crib which looks more like an altar. This may well have linked the nativity with the future death of this child and the Eucharist in which that death is brought home to participants in the Church. Its position in the picture also recalls the idea that Christ is the cornerstone of the Church. The major theme is God made man but other themes are part of the whole picture. The advantage of pictures like this is that the whole and the parts can be seen at the same time, unlike the telling of a narrative, although narratives need to be known in order to interpret the picture.

Another example of these multi-dimensional presentations is Piero della Francesca's *The Baptism of Christ* [1448–50] in the National Gallery. We see Jesus standing in the centre while John the Baptist pours water over him. Above him the Holy Spirit in the form of a dove is coming upon him as the Gospels tell the story. Beside Jesus is a tree. This tree recalls the Tree of Life in the Garden of Eden and may hint at the Cross. The Tree of Life was forfeited by Adam and Eve but Jesus has come to make its fruit available, even though it will cost him his life on the Cross. In the painting Jesus is standing on dry ground recalling the Israelites crossing the Jordan to enter the Promised Land. Behind John another candidate prepares for baptism. This indicates that Jesus stood in the place of human beings and invites others to follow him. There are figures dressed like the magi of the nativity in the background. Some writers see the three angels to the left of the tree as a reminder of the Trinity. In the distance is the hint of a city, perhaps Jerusalem. And all of this is set in a 15th century Italian Renaissance setting showing its relevance to the artist's time.

The Cross

The most widely recognized symbol of Christianity is the Cross. Part of the Celtic legacy in Wales, Scotland and Ireland are stone crosses with the arms and upright of the Cross linked by arcs of a circle. This suggests the Cross surrounded by a wreath of victory, much as Constantine's soldiers had the *chi-rho* sign surrounded by a wreath. Certainly the earlier representations of Christ on the Cross show him alive and reigning as it were from the Cross. This can be seen in the second of four 5th century reliefs on four sides of a casket in the British Museum. It encourages the viewer to be reminded that Christ opened the Gates of Paradise not only to the thief crucified beside him, but to every believer. Such pictures stressed the divinity of Christ. Only as the Chalcedon formulae became established and widely accepted did people feel able to portray a more human Jesus and one who suffered excruciating agony for the human race. A 13th century panel known as the *Man of Sorrows*, one half of a diptych, in the National Gallery illustrates this trend. But it is still in the rather stylized, almost abstract Byzantine style. The following centuries produced the more realistically human Jesus. Giotto's early 14th century paintings were strikingly lifelike and realistic.

This trend reached a climax in Grunewald's dramatic altarpiece for the monastery at Isenheim in Alsace which was completed by 1516. It was a complex structure which included a number of different pictures, some of which were folded inside the others. In the closed position viewers saw the Crucifixion scene flanked by pictures of two saints. It is a striking image. The flesh of Christ has been ripped by the lashes and reflects that of people dying from a plague called 'burning sickness'. The crown of thorns has long, sharp spikes. The body is twisted with agony and blood flows from a wound in his side. Mary is fainting into the arms of the disciple John while Mary Magdalene weeps on her knees at the foot of the Cross. On the other side of the Cross is John the Baptist pointing to Jesus, the Lamb of God, who is dying to take away the sins of the world. Any human being suffering from the plague, who contemplated this picture, would have realized that Christ himself understood what suffering was like, from his own experience. When the two hinged panels on which the Crucifixion is painted are opened out they reveal three brilliantly bright pictures inside: one of the Annunciation, one of the Nativity and a dramatic, dazzling Resurrection scene. The rising Christ is seen in a large halo of golden light. Here is Jesus not only restored but glorified as three disciples had once seen him on the Mount of Transfiguration. This is the victory of light over darkness. Those who came for Mass to this altar were confronted with the extremes of suffering, self-sacrifice and hope.

Who is this?

Pictures of Christ often included the Virgin Mary, sometimes with the Christ Child sitting on her lap as if enthroned, sometimes breastfeeding the child, so illustrating his two natures. There were also many pictures of saints. The Virgin and the saints were regarded as people who had got very close to Jesus and so might speak a word for less worthy worshippers.

In the summer of 2005 England's oldest altarpiece went on display at the National Gallery in London. It is a large altar panel probably painted for the restoration of Westminster Abbey in 1269. It is divided into five panels. In the centre Christ holds a beautiful miniature representation of the Earth which includes the Sun and Moon, water, a boat, sheep and birds. He holds the whole world in his hand. This is in striking contrast to Italian altarpieces of this period which show Christ on the Cross. Also unusual are scenes depicting the miracles of Christ, the raising of Jairus' daughter, the healing of the man born blind and the feeding of the five thousand.

PILGRIMAGES AND PROCESSIONS

Places associated with the Virgin and saints, or with particular icons of them, became centres of pilgrimage as did the holy places where Jesus had actually been. At the end of the 4th century, Egeria, a wealthy Spanish nun, was in Jerusalem for Easter and she wrote about the excitement of being in the very sites where the events of Christ's sufferings took place. She saw a piece of the Cross which was kept in a silver casket but taken out and put on the table while people went forward to kiss it. Then for the three hours during which Jesus was on the Cross the crowds listened to readings from the prophets and the Gospels about the sufferings of the Lord. These were interspersed with prayers. 'The emotion shown and the mourning by all the people at every lesson and prayer is wonderful; for there is none, neither great or small, who, on that day during those three hours, does not lament more than can be conceived, that the Lord had suffered those things for us.' This vividly illustrates the reality of the sufferings of Jesus for these pilgrims and their understanding that he had died for them. Unfortunately this also illustrates the rather superstitious veneration of relics. It was said that eventually there came to be enough pieces of the Cross at different churches across Europe to make a whole forest. These and things like the blood of Christ or body parts of the saints came to be what drew crowds of pilgrims to various centres of pilgrimage.

Processions along the Via Dolorosa, the route that Jesus had taken to the Cross, stopping at the Stations of the Cross to reflect on those momentous events, were copied in churches and cities across Europe. Sometimes there were seven stations, or twelve, or in more recent years fourteen, but at each a picture or carving recalled a particular incident on the way to the Cross and the tomb. Other processions on Palm Sunday or various feast days or following a statue of the Virgin Mary were ways of concretely bringing the gospel of Jesus alive to ordinary people. The most important procession was the one on the feast of Corpus Christi (the Body of Christ), to honour the Lord's Supper or Eucharist. The bishop carried a silver container called a monstrance (a casket) to show the bread of the sacrament to the people. These were dramatic means of advertising the gospel and pointing to Jesus as the centre of the devotion of vast numbers of the population. Inevitably economic, social and political interests exploited these religious needs so that these events were far from pure devotion to Jesus. The Crusades developed out of pilgrimages to these holy places.

MIRACLE PLAYS, MUSIC AND POETRY
Other dramatic ways of presenting Jesus to people were the miracle or mystery plays. Scenes from the Bible or legends of the saints were acted in the open air, often on carts and put on by town guilds. The most popular subject was the Passion of Christ but other incidents from the stories of his life were also performed.

Sometimes the whole story from Creation to the Last Judgment was divided up into a sequence or cycle of plays with particular pageants allocated to appropriate guilds. So, for example, the Bakers performed *The Last Supper*, the Pinners [nail makers] *The Crucifixion* and the Butchers *The Death of Christ*. The oldest and best preserved of these mystery plays are those from York which date from the second half of the 14th century when the city had recovered from the Black Death of 1349. Some of Jesus' speeches are very moving. For example, in *The Death of Christ*, Jesus speaks from the Cross. He says:

> With intense suffering have I paid like this to heal thy sin.
>
> Never cease to look on me, how willingly I bend [surrender?] my body.
>
> No one in this world could imagine what sorrow I suffer for you.
>
> Make sure my kindness is well known.
>
> Take me as your true home and trust for foxes have their dens and birds their nests but the Son of Man today has nowhere to rest his head.

The Chester mystery cycle includes the story of the offerings of the three kings who came to visit the infant Jesus. They explain why they have brought their particular gifts. The first king brings gold to acknowledge that Jesus is a king and to help his poor mother. The second king brings incense to make the stable smell better and because it is associated with worship of God and prayer. Myrrh is to anoint him and points to his death and burial.

Thus shall we honour him all three

with things that falls to his degree,

touching manhood and deity.

(Ford, p. 159)

As each king follows the others he adds further layers of explanation acknowledging Jesus as Lord and 'Conqueror of all Mankind'.

Miracle plays were often accompanied by music but they were not the only use of music and poetry. Hildegard, Abbess of Rupertsberg, near Bingen [1098–1179], in the Rhineland, among her many writings included music and poetry of a mystical kind. Of Mary she wrote:

O most radiant mother of sacred healing

you poured ointments through your holy son

on the sobbing wounds of death

that Eve built into torment for souls.

(Miles, p. 151)

Here is a complex mixture of images apparently attributing to Mary the initiative in saving people from the consequences of Eve's sin. Jesus, her holy son, is the means of her salvation. A 9th century German epic *Heliand* told many of the Gospel stories in Old Saxon verse. It portrayed Christ as the Saviour leading his Apostles into battle like a great Germanic leader. The author could not accept the humility of Jesus which led him to ride into Jerusalem on a donkey nor the teaching of Jesus on not resisting your enemy. This was not the only time Jesus was captured by a culture and distorted in the process.

MONKS, FRIARS AND MYSTICS

From the early centuries of the Christian Church, some people had withdrawn from life in towns and cities to the desert in their quest for God and for holiness. After all, the desert was where God had met with Moses and where Jesus had defeated the Devil before he began his ministry. At first these people were solitary hermits but later they banded together in communities for mutual protection and encouragement. The incentive to both men and women to withdraw into spiritual communities was stimulated by the increasing preoccupation of the churches, east and west, with politics and what we might call secular concerns. When Gregory the Great [540–604 CE] reluctantly left the monastery to become pope he wrote, 'But now all the beauty of that spiritual repose is gone and the contact with worldly men and their affairs, which is a necessary part of my duties as a bishop, has left my soul defiled with earthly cares.'

Inevitably life in the monasteries was not always what it should have been and reforms and new rules were introduced from time to time. According to the Rule of St Benedict, one of the most widely followed sets of rules, the purpose of monastic life was to learn how to renounce oneself to follow Christ and share in the Passion of Christ. The means to this end were private prayer, manual labour and communal prayer. Christ himself was the model for the three vows of poverty, chastity and obedience. Monks were 'not to value anything more highly than the love of Christ.' Bernard of Clairvaux [1090–1153], a Cistercian monk, taught people to focus on love for Christ by contemplating stories of what he did in his life and ministry. Bernard said that people who visualized that they were present and involved in the stories would receive salvation. In one of his sermons for Christmas Eve, he makes the point that the Saviour *is* born, not 'was', saying that on the following day, 'We shall see majesty in humility, power in weakness, God in man.' The chorale 'O sacred head sore wounded' so memorably set in Bach's *St Matthew's Passion* is attributed to Bernard of Clairvaux and demonstrates the kind of meditation on the Passion which he taught.

The friars

In the 12th century there emerged brotherhoods of itinerant friars, the most famous of whom was St Francis of Assissi [1181–1226]. He was the son of a wealthy merchant who took Jesus' words to the rich young man in the Gospels literally. He gave up his riches and began to preach and live the simple life of poverty. When he was joined by some followers their lifestyle was based on Jesus' instructions to the twelve when he sent them out on mission. They took nothing with them but depended on the hospitality they were offered. He was joined by St Clare of Assissi, who at the age of 18 became the remarkable leader of an order of nuns called the 'Poor Clares'. They lived at the small church of San Damiano striving to achieve what she called 'the privilege of poverty', which meant living without land or regular income. Like Bernard before him, Francis was concerned that people should let the story of Jesus move them to love, compassion, joy and grief. So he would walk along wailing for the sufferings of Jesus and others joined him. He believed that the living Christ was to be found in the poor as he had encountered him in a leper. He so identified himself with Jesus that he denied himself food, shelter and sleep. He spoke of Jesus as one poor at his birth, poor in his ministry and poor at his death.

In 1223 in the small town of Greccio he suggested the construction of the first Christmas crib to show people the birth of the poor King. This led to a new realism in painting and poetry proclaiming that in the suffering and death of Jesus the mystery of both divine and human life was seen. He also had a remarkable experience in which he received the marks of the crucified Jesus [the stigmata] in his hands, feet and side. Pope Pius XI was to call him 'the second Christ'. Bernard was a great preacher and Francis an activist. Both were also men of prayer and deep spirituality.

The mystics

Another aspect of medieval spirituality was mysticism. The word 'mysticism' is interesting because it suggests an experience which cannot be spoken about in words and yet many of the mystics wrote about their experiences sometimes in rather extraordinary terms. The female mystic Julian of Norwich [*c.* 1342–1413 CE], for example, when she was seriously ill, received a series of visions on which she wrote her subsequent reflections. As she looked at a crucifix she saw a vision of the crucified Christ with blood trickling down his face from the crown of thorns. It is significant to recall that the times in which she lived were times of war and plague. The Black Death visited Norwich three times in her lifetime. But through her reflections on these visions she was overwhelmed by the love of God. Her pain left her. She speaks of Christ as 'our Mother'. To take three sample quotations:

> Jesus is our true Mother in nature by our first creation and
> he is our true Mother in grace by his taking our created nature.

We know that all our mothers bear us for pain and
death. What is that? But our true Mother Jesus, he alone
bears us for joy and for endless life.

This blessed friend is Jesus; it is his will and plan that
we hang on to him and hold tight always, in whatever
circumstances; for whether we are filthy or clean is all the
same to his love.

(Showings/Revelations, Chapters 59 and 60)

It is clear that Julian uses the term 'Mother' metaphorically
to speak of Jesus as the one who gives birth to those who are
born again. He suffers for them, nourishes, protects and teaches,
just like a human mother. But in times of death and suffering how
important it was to have such a one to hold on to, someone who
loves. Jesus on the Cross tells us how deeply he loves us and, in
the style of Augustine of Hippo, Julian says if you had been the
only one who needed him he would still have come for you. She
says that in this life we are to suffer with him on the Cross in our
pain, sorrow and dying, yet this will all be changed when we are
with him in Heaven.

Mysticism is sometimes defined in terms of an experience of
immediate union with God and Julian's writing about the soul as
the divine reality which unites us to God has been taken to claim
that she shared the same kind of mysticism as Hindus for example.
But they speak of the individual being lost in *Brahman* [Ultimate
Reality] like a drop of water being lost in the ocean. For Julian
oneness with God and with Jesus was the hope for the future and
seems to retain the identity of the person. For the present sin and
partial knowledge prevent that union:

> For until I am substantially oned to him, I may never have full
> rest nor true bliss. That is to say, until I be so fastened to him
> that there is nothing that is made between my God and me.
>
> (*Showings*, Chapter 5)

Thomas à Kempis [1380–1471 CE] entered a monastery at the age of 20 and stayed there until he died aged 90. He is usually credited with writing one of the most popular devotional books of all time, *The Imitation of Christ*. This book understands the relationship between Christ and the individual in terms of friendship, and of union with the Godhead through the sacrament of the Eucharist:

> When Jesus is near, all is well and nothing seems difficult.
> When He is absent, all is hard. When Jesus does not speak
> within, all other comfort is empty, but if He says only a
> word, it brings great consolation . . . Of all those who are
> dear to you, let Him be your special love. Let all things be
> loved for the sake of Jesus, but Jesus for His own sake.
> Jesus Christ must be loved alone with a special love, for
> He alone, of all friends, is good and faithful.
>
> Love Him, therefore, and keep Him as your friend; for
> when all others desert you, He will not abandon you, nor
> allow you to perish at the last. Whether you wish it or
> not, you must in the end be parted from them all.
>
> Hold fast to Jesus, both in life and death, and trust your-
> self to His faithfulness, for He alone can aid you when all
> others fail . . . He desires your heart for Himself alone,
> and to reign there as King on His throne.
>
> (*Imitation* Book 2, Chapter 8)

At the same time Thomas knew that real Christian discipleship included a cross. 'Jesus has always many who love His heavenly kingdom, but few who bear His Cross.' He elaborated this into a critique of those who love Jesus for what they can get. 'Seldom is anyone so spiritual as to strip himself entirely of self-love.' All of this speaks of deep personal and individual devotion to Jesus and Thomas discusses many practical implications for day to day living and dealing with other people. Jesus is not a figure of the past but a companion in the present and a hope for the future for people like Thomas.

THEOLOGIANS

There is a clear overlap between theologians and the monks, friars and mystics for many of the theologians spent years in monasteries or abbeys or were themselves friars or mystics.

In the Eastern Church

Following the iconoclastic controversies, the two outstanding theologians were men in the mystical tradition. They were Symeon [949–1022 CE] and Gregory Palamas, Archbishop of Thessalonica [1296–1359 CE]. Their theology was experiential and poetic rather than rational and systematic. They were conscious of dealing with mysteries beyond the straightforward use of words. The main subjects of their poetry are the nearness, yet otherness of God, the Holy Spirit and the Divine Light. 'He is in my heart, he is in Heaven' [Symeon]. Through the Spirit, every Christian could encounter Christ in a vision of Divine Light. But this light was frequently only refracted through the darkness and brokenness of human pain and suffering. Of Jesus, Symeon wrote without qualification, 'Christ my God'. Gregory taught people how to achieve

---

THE JESUS PRAYER

The Jesus Prayer was the repetition of the name 'Lord Jesus' or in its fuller form, 'Lord Jesus Christ, Son of God, have mercy on me a sinner'. This was understood to 'practise the presence of Jesus' and lead the individual to love of the Lord and union with God through purification.

---

inner stillness through repeating the Jesus prayer and controlled breathing. He justified this on the basis that by his incarnation Christ had 'made the flesh an inexhaustible source of sanctification'. 'Sanctification' means 'making holy' or 'sharing the nature of God'. This was the same kind of argument which had been used to support the use of icons. Now it was applied to human beings.

In the Western church

In the West, theologians were more frequently teachers in the cathedral schools and the new universities. The questions they addressed were still about the nature, or essence, of Jesus but they tended, as time went by, to discuss in more detail how the death of Jesus saved people. Before the Council of Chalcedon, Augustine had written, in his *Confessions,* that Jesus Christ the man was the true Mediator between God and human beings. Like people he was mortal and died. Like God he was just, 'and because the reward of the just is life and peace, he, through his righteousness with God, nullified the death of the wicked by choosing to share their death' [10.43]. People were saved through faith in his death. Augustine distinguished Jesus as the Word of God, and as the Word of God incarnate. As the Word of God 'he is equal with God' for only God can save. As the Word of God incarnate, Jesus is a teacher of infinite wisdom and leads people to God. He also shows them how to live and gives them hope of eternal life. He is the new head of the human race. Those who are united with him in his Church now will one day be with him in glory. Later writers were often indebted to Augustine but wanted to probe parts of his explanation more deeply.

Anselm

Anselm [1033–1109], Archbishop of Canterbury, wrote a book called *Cur Deus homo?* (*Why did God become a human being?*). In this book he tried to explain the death of Christ in terms of 'satisfaction', an idea taken from Roman law. 'Every sin must be followed either by satisfaction or by punishment.'

Satisfaction required three things:

- that people stop sinning,
- they seek pardon,
- something more must be done, to compensate God for the injury done to his honour.

The background to Anselm's idea was the feudal system which was the way society was organized in much of Europe at that time. In Anselm's view God is the King. Sin is an offence to his honour. But since God is infinite only something of infinite value could compensate for the injury done to him. This was something no ordinary human being could pay. Therefore someone whose life was of infinite value and who had no sin of his own had freely to offer his life for the sins of the world. This explained why God became man in Jesus Christ.

THE FEUDAL SYSTEM

This was a system based on land. From 1265 onwards in England lords held land from the king in return for which they would answer his summons to battle or 'parliament'. They then let land out to their men ('vassals') in return for goods and services. In this system it was the duty of the vassals to uphold the honour of their lord as the lord was required to uphold the honour of the king.

This offered an explanation both of the incarnation and the Cross in terms which made sense in that society. But in feudal society the king, the lords and the vassals were all subject to the rule of law, an abstract system of justice which was greater than them all. Was God also somehow bound by such a system of law? Could he not forgive without demanding something in return?

Abelard

Abelard [1079–1142] was a brilliant 12th century French philosopher whose career was tragically cut short by the tempestous saga of his love affair with Heloise. He retired first to a monastery and then to an abbey. Later he resumed his work until he was condemned for heresy. He died in a priory at Cluny. His explanation of the death of Christ was both simpler and on the face of it more appealing. He argued that the Cross was a revelation of divine love and of such great love that it inspired human beings to respond by loving God. He said, 'our redemption is the great love awakened in us by the Passion of Jesus.' Such love also inspired people to live new lives and this was made possible by the Holy Spirit.

There is no doubt that there is some important truth here, but when compared with the New Testament writings, it is only one dimension of the story, a partial account.

Aquinas

Thomas Aquinas [1225–1275] was a Dominican friar, lecturer and writer. His greatest work was his incomplete *Summa Theologica* [*Summary of Theology*]. His discussion of Jesus is found principally in Book III. Aquinas said that the primary reason for the incarnation was to deal with human sin. 'If there was no sin, the incarnation would not have taken place' [1.3]. Jesus was the perfect human being, the personal union of the Word of God and human nature. Through grace he has the power to perfect those who are members of his body, the Church. When Aquinas said that Jesus knew everything in his divine nature so that he lived by sight, not by faith, he put in question the humanity of Jesus. But as Mediator, Jesus fulfilled the roles of priest, prophet and king. When Aquinas discusses the Passion of Christ he does not follow Anselm and claim that the satisfaction of God's honour was necessary, but he agrees that it was appropriate. The death of Christ was a sacrifice, inspired by love, to honour God and to turn away his wrath. Not that this made God love people again as if he had stopped loving them. He had never stopped loving them. His love is everlasting. It is people who are changed by the washing away of sin and the offering of 'satisfaction'. Christ suffered the punishment due to sinful human beings and delivered them from the Devil's captivity through the victory of God. Aquinas deals with the Resurrection at length for the Resurrection of Jesus is both the example and the cause of the Resurrection of those who believe in him. In this way sin is destroyed and human beings are restored to God and human dignity.

This account is sometimes criticized for separating the salvation of human beings from the renewal of creation which is also part of the New Testament picture. In using Anselm's idea of 'satisfaction' Aquinas also reflected medieval feudalism.

Devotion to Jesus Christ

So how does all this contribute to people's ideas of the essence of Jesus in the period from the 5th to the 15th centuries? Pictures and icons encouraged devotion to Jesus and show how stories and ideas about him were 'translated' in a changing world. They enabled stories to be seen and in the case of icons provided a point of contact with the spiritual world. This quest for real, tangible evidence and participation in the sacred events described in the gospels was also the motivation behind pilgrimages, processions and miracle plays. At times, as we have seen, Jesus was accommodated to popular values and legends which distorted the teaching of the gospels but this was entertainment as well as religious education. The inner quest for real contact with Jesus and the desire to live according to his teachings often prompted people to go into monasteries or nunneries. To know him directly as a friend in the present led people to prize the writings of the mystics who seemed to have progressed to experiences beyond the ordinary. The theologians tried to articulate this faith even if they sometimes dealt with mysteries beyond words. Aquinas brought the disciplines of Aristotelian philosophy to bear on his arguments for the existence of God and this rational framework was a tool for his thinking about Christ. But, as we saw at the beginning of this chapter, by the 15th century people were moving into a new world.

Chapter 6

Jesus in word
and sacrament

Towards the end of the Middle Ages, there was mounting criticism
of the popes and bishops of the Catholic Church which eventually came to a climax in the Protestant Reformation and the Catholic
response of the Counter-Reformation. Within this context a significant shift occurred in the churches of the reformers from the
centrality of the Mass or Eucharist to the sermon as an exposition
of scripture. For three hundred years preaching was one of the
principal means of shaping public opinion and promoting elemen-
tary education about the Christian faith. In addition Protestant
scholars gave themselves to the task of translating the Bible into
the language of the people whether that was German, French,
English or the native languages of the Amerindians. The number
of sacraments among the Protestants was reduced from the
Catholic seven to the two ordained by Jesus himself: baptism and
the Eucharist. It is appropriate then to speak of Jesus in word and
sacraments. At the same time words spoken from the pulpit
continued to be supported, or challenged, by artistic works and

as the 16th century moved into the 17th drama and poetry flourished. Not all of this was devoted to Jesus, but some of the most
powerful words were.

Jan Hus

Any visitor to the beautiful city of Prague who is given a guided
tour will be introduced to the magnificent memorial of Jan Hus
[1370–1415]. He was burned as a heretic in 1415 on the orders
of the Council of Constance. The guide will sometimes point out
that here is evidence that the Reformation began in Bohemia
over a century before Martin Luther took his famous stand in
Germany. Certainly Hus and his followers raised the cause of the
reformation of the Church and the movement was difficult to
suppress. One could rightly point out that Hus himself was a
follower of John Wyclif, the Oxford scholar who had already
inspired Lollard preachers, laymen who toured England with
their strong criticisms of the official Church. Wyclif also inspired
friends and colleagues to produce one of the first translations
of the whole Bible intothe English of their time. Both Hus and
Wyclif contrasted the lavish, powerful lifestyle of the bishops and
wealthy clericswith the poverty and powerlessness of Jesus 'the
poor King of the poor'. Hus had a passion for Christ as the
embodiment of truth, that is, truth understood as faithfulness
or loyalty to God's covenant with human beings. He held that
Jesus Christ was the one true head of the Church and that the
Church depended on its relationship with him. When Church
leaders claimed authority for themselves they were in error and
the Church needed to be reformed.

Hus was a powerful preacher in the Bethlehem Chapel of the University of Prague. His preaching was like that of the Lollards, itinerant preachers who continued to make their presence felt for the next century and further. Preaching the message of Jesus made the gospel known to ordinary folk who could not read for themselves. Dominican and Franciscan friars were also travelling preachers encouraging people to live more like Jesus and according to his teaching.

Then came the invention of printing. Now thousands of copies of sermons were printed and distributed and the influence of particular 'heretics' was much more difficult to contain. Bibles, lectures, tracts, and handbooks for teaching Christian faith and practice, flooded the markets and were smuggled into countries where the authorities tried to keep them out. The preached word tended to push the sacraments into second place in Christian worship and people argued about what actually happens in the Eucharist. The Catholic Church believed that the bread and wine became the body and blood of Christ. To receive the bread or the wine was to receive Christ. Lay people were given the bread but priests had bread and wine. For reformers, like Hus and their followers, the Lord's Supper should be celebrated with bread and wine for all. It was a ritual in which all participated equally. This threatened to undermine the privileges and prestige of the clergy, especially when Hus appealed to the common people to take reform into their own hands. But Hus was burned and the pope ordered a series of crusades against Bohemia to restore the churches to Catholic ways. The Husites were not eliminated but the cause of reform was not seriously addressed until the protests of Martin Luther.

Martin Luther

It may well be true, as recent writers have claimed, that the whole faculty at the University of Wittenberg was involved in the Reformation but Martin Luther [1483–1546] was clearly the figurehead on the European stage. But Luther did not see himself as a revolutionary. He thought of himself as a faithful and obedient servant of the Church. He was totally opposed to the idea of breaking away from the Catholic Church and was very distressed when people called themselves Lutherans. He saw himself called to be a university lecturer in Biblical Studies, appointed to expound the Scriptures, and this he did. He also wrote many tracts and preached many sermons which were circulated in print. In his desire to make the Bible as widely read and known as possible he gave himself to the work of translating it into German.

Jesus the judge

Luther had entered an Augustinian monastery at Erfurt in 1505 where he subjected himself to a strict regime of prayer, fasting and sleepless nights, in his search for God. As far as Jesus was concerned he feared him as a 'terrible judge, the painted kind that one sees in paintings sitting on a rainbow'. 'I knew Christ as none other than a stern judge, from whose face I wanted to flee and yet could not.' The crux of the matter was that God, being the righteous God he was, would deal with people according to their deserts. This was true even when the righteousness of God was understood as his faithfulness to his promises, for his covenant was understood to mean that he would show grace to those who deserved it. The trouble was that no one could know if they deserved it. 'Who can love a God who wants to deal with sinners with justice?' He was filled with dread and a sense of doom. His Father Confessor Staupitz told him to meditate on the wounds of Jesus.

The good news

Luther came to see that Christ was the key. Near the end of his life, in a famous autobiographical fragment, he gave some account of his 'discovery'. It involved a new understanding of the phrase 'the righteousness of God'. Pondering the words of St Paul in Romans 1:17 'the righteousness of God is revealed in it [that is, the gospel], as it is written: the righteous shall live by faith', he says, 'I began to understand that 'righteousness of God' as that by which the righteous lives by the gift of God, namely by faith . . . This immediately made me feel as though I had been born again and as though I had entered through open gates into paradise itself.' He goes on to say that he now compared this phrase 'the righteousness of God' with others such as 'the work of God', 'the power of God', 'the wisdom of God', 'the strength of God', 'the salvation of God' and 'the glory of God'. Each of these described something which God does in the lives of human beings. So the same must be true of 'the righteousness of God'. Luther called it an 'alien righteousness' meaning a righteousness which belongs to somebody else. That somebody else was Christ. Luther speaks of a 'sweet exchange' between Jesus Christ and the sinner.

> Therefore, my dear brother, learn Christ and Him cruci-
> fied; learn to pray to Him despairing of yourself, saying,
> "You, Lord Jesus, are my righteousness and I am Your sin;

> You have taken on Yourself what You were not, and You
> have given to me what I am not."
>
> (George, pp. 69–70)

One of Luther's great themes was that Christ is for us, on our
side. Christ became a human being at the incarnation for us.
On the Cross he suffered and defeated sin and death, God's
wrath and the curse, all for us. Faith takes hold of, and relies
on this. The believer is then united with Christ, forgiven and
reconciled to God. By his Spirit, Christ lives within believers
and changes them, giving them new life.

This is the gospel of salvation. It works through the preaching
of the word, that is the message of the gospel, and the sacraments.
Luther understood the preaching of the story of Jesus to include
the account of his Incarnation, death, Resurrection and present
rule as Lord. As people heard this gospel preached, they heard
God making promises which they could accept with grateful trust.
Hearing the message preached was itself an encounter with Jesus
Christ, and when this was received by faith, it led to being united
with him. As Luther's friend Melanchthon wrote, 'God wishes to
be known in a new way (i.e. through the foolishness of preaching).'
It was the preaching of the Word rather than the administration
of the sacraments which Luther saw as the chief mission of
the Church.

The Sacraments

Luther came to accept only two sacraments, baptism and the
Eucharist, as those authorized by Christ. They were visible words
of God holding out the same promises as the word preached and

---

WHAT ARE THE SACRAMENTS?

A sacrament is the use of a material object like bread, wine or water to signify the act of God's blessing before those who are about to receive Him. The object must bear some resemblance to the object or concept being signified and its use has to be properly authorized.

---

to be personally received in a similar way, by faith. A sacrament was a lantern. 'It points to Christ and his image, enabling you to say when faced by the image of death, sin and hell, "God promised and in his Sacraments he gave me a sure sign of his grace."' (George, pp. 93–94)

Luther accepted infant baptism as the Christian equivalent to circumcision and thus as a mark of inclusion into God's covenant with His people. To those who questioned whether the baby had faith Luther argued that God gave that faith and nothing so clearly underlined that salvation was by grace alone.

But it was over the Eucharist that the most intense disagreements occurred among the reformers because people thought the gospel itself was at stake. The Catholic Church had retained 'the sacrifice of the Mass' as the central act of Christian worship. Luther denied Catholic teaching that the substance of the bread and wine changed into the body and blood of Christ but he agreed that Christ was truly present. The words of Jesus, 'This is my body' guaranteed his presence. In this Luther did not go as far as some reformers wanted. The classical confrontation took place between Luther and the Swiss Reformer Ulrich Zwingli at Marburg in 1529.

THE MASS

The word 'Mass' comes from the Latin word meaning 'dismissal' and refers to the closing blessing at the end of the service. The latter is an adaptation of the Last Supper rite which Jesus shared with the twelve Apostles 'the night before he was betrayed'. Jesus' key words, spoken when he broke the bread ('This is my body'), and when he poured the wine ('This is my blood') are still echoed in the Eucharistic rite in churches the world over today. These days priests offer the sacrifice of Christ to believers in the form of bread and wine for the forgiveness of their sins, as relevant today as it was back then.

Luther and Zwingli agreed on some things. They both thought that the whole congregation should take part in the Eucharist, not the priests alone. They both wanted the Scriptures read and preached. They both rejected the idea that this was the sacrifice of the Mass and that the bread and the wine were miraculously transformed in some way. But Luther wanted to insist that Christ was mysteriously present in the elements. His key text was the words of Jesus, 'This is my body' which he refused to allow Zwingli to interpret in the form, 'This signifies my body'. For Luther a symbol contained what it signified. For Zwingli, Luther was wrong to connect the eating of Christ's body with the forgiveness of sins. For him the words expressed the acceptance of Christ's death by faith. There was a metaphorical as well as a literal sense of eating. They also argued about where Christ was. For Zwingli he was in Heaven. The Eucharist was consequently a memorial of Christ's death. Luther argued that Christ was everywhere and therefore present not only in Heaven but on all Christian altars. He was stressing Christ's divine nature, whereas Zwingli was more influenced by his human nature although neither would have denied the Chalcedonian definition that in Christ two natures, human and divine, were united in one person.

One observer commented that, 'Future generations will laugh at the pleasure our age takes in quarrelling when we raise such a disturbance about the very signs which should unite us' (George, p. 144), but the participants believed that the foundations of their faith, particularly their understanding of Jesus, and the meaning of his words, were at stake. For Luther the Eucharist was an extension of the incarnation. Christ had returned to Heaven but he had also continued to be present with his followers and especially present according to his word in the Eucharist. For Zwingli the bread and the wine pointed to the historical death of Christ on the Cross. It was there the decisive action had taken place for salvation. The Eucharist recalled these events to the present faith of believers. They could not agree and these two understandings continued in the churches after their deaths.

Ulrich Zwingli

Zwingli [1484–1531] was a scholar who had gained a great reputation as a preacher. For this reason when the post of people's priest at the Great Minster in Zurich became vacant he was called to take over at the end of 1518. He was strongly influenced by the Dutch Renaissance scholar Erasmus, who in his desire to get back to the sources of Christianity had published a critical edition of the Greek New Testament. Zwingli had also read some of Luther's works. He began his ministry by preaching through the Gospel of Matthew. As one observer commented of Zwingli:

> He praised God the Father, and taught men to trust only in the Son of God, Jesus Christ, as saviour. He vehemently denounced all unbelief, superstition and hypocrisy. Eagerly he strove after repentance, improvement of life, and Christian love and faith.
>
> (Atkinson, p. 139)

People crowded in to hear this preaching and Zwingli preached in the marketplace on Fridays so that those who had come in from the villages could hear him. For all his differences from Luther over the Eucharist both of them were committed to bringing Jesus to people in the preaching of the Word. This was now the heart of Church worship and Church life. The pulpit was more important than the altar, which many now called the table. Zwingli's life and ministry were cut short by his death as a chaplain on the field of battle. But a Frenchman, Jean Calvin, would take over the leadership of the Reformation in Switzerland.

John Calvin

Like Luther, John Calvin [1509–64] reflected on his conversion much later in life. His own account runs, 'At first, although I was so obstinately given to the superstitions of the papacy that it was extremely difficult to drag me from the depths of the mire, yet by a sudden conversion He tamed my heart and made it teachable, this heart which for its age was excessively hardened in such matters' [*Commentary on the Psalms*, 1558]. It is significant that Calvin attributed his conversion to God and that God had made him teachable. These were the key elements in Calvin's understanding of Christian discipleship, for a disciple was someone who could be taught. The best-known of Calvin's works is his *Institutes of the Christian Religion* which was published in various editions during his lifetime. We can assume that this was the ground base of his preaching.

Calvin's understanding of Jesus

Also like Luther, Calvin's thinking was centred on Jesus Christ. The purpose of the whole Bible was to bear witness to Christ. He accepted from the early Church Councils the teaching about the two natures of Christ and their union in one person. As Mediator between God and human beings Christ had to be truly God and truly man; 'since neither as God alone could he feel death, nor as man alone could he overcome it, he coupled human nature with divine that to atone for sin he might submit the weakness of the one to death; and that, wrestling with death by the power of the other nature, he might win victory for us' (*Institutes* Bk II.12.3). Without such a Mediator human beings could never approach God. This was true before as well as after the Fall of Adam and Eve. But sin had made the situation worse – making human beings a horror to God and filling them with hate and fear for God so that they only wanted to run away from him. So the Son of God had to become a human being that he might willingly share human poverty and misery, fear and sadness, death and despair. He shared their experience that they might share his and become children of God.

Calvin explained the work of Christ in terms of the roles of prophet, king and priest. As prophet, Christ was anointed by the Spirit to proclaim the gospel of the grace of God's kingdom. As king, he exercised the sovereignty of God, even on the Cross giving the repentant thief access to his kingdom. That man had asked the dying Jesus to remember him when he came into his kingdom. Jesus had replied, 'Today you will be with me in Paradise', a word which meant walking in the royal gardens. As priest, he had offered the perfect sacrifice of himself to turn away the wrath of God and make perfect satisfaction for sins.

> However much we may be sinners by our own fault, we nevertheless remain his [the Lord's] creatures. However much we have brought death upon ourselves, yet he has created us unto life. Thus he is moved by pure and freely given love of us to receive us into grace. Since there is a perpetual and irreconcilable disagreement between righteousness and unrighteousness, so long as we remain sinners he cannot receive us completely. Therefore, to take away all cause for enmity and to reconcile us utterly to himself, he wipes out all evil in us by the expiation set forth in the death of Christ; that we, who were previously unclean and impure, may show ourselves righteous and holy in his sight.
>
> (*Institutes*, Bk II.16.3)

Unlike Anselm, Calvin thought that God could have chosen another way to save human beings, but said that this was in fact the way that he demonstrated his grace and love towards them. And this way entailed certain requirements. The 'penalty to which we were subject, [was] imposed on this righteous man . . . to make satisfaction for our redemption a form of death had to be chosen in which he might free us both by transferring our condemnation to himself and by taking our guilt upon himself' (*Institutes*, Bk II.16.5). People were called to respond to his death by a radical change of life; dead to the past, to live in new ways.

The Sacraments

But what did Calvin teach about the Sacraments? For him, they were one of the three ways in which God graciously communicated with His people. He spoke through his Word, confirmed the Word in the Sacraments and by the Spirit 'opens a way into our hearts for his Word and Sacraments. Else they would merely beat on our ears and meet our sight without at all affecting us inwardly'. He defined a sacrament as 'an outward sign by which the Lord seals on our consciences the promises of his good will toward us in order to sustain the weakness of our faith; and we, in turn, attest our piety toward him in the presence of the Lord and of his angels and before men' (*Institutes*, Bk IV.14.1). In the Sacraments, the Lord gave the thing promised and signified. On the one hand baptism was more than a sign that people belonged to the Church or to Christ.

> Those who have dared to write that baptism is nothing but a mark and sign, by which we profess our religion before men, as a man-at-arms puts on the uniform of his prince to show whom he serves, have not considered the principal thing about baptism — that is, that we have to take it with this promise, that all those who believe and are baptized will be saved.
>
> (*Institutes*, Bk IV.15.1)

On the other hand, there was nothing magical or purifying about the water. Only the blood (that is, the death) of Christ purifies. Baptism was a symbol of the cleansing and gift of the purity of Christ, and in baptism, Christ united the believer with his death and Resurrection. Calvin said that infants had a right to be baptized under the new covenant as under the old covenant they were circumcised. The difference was in externals only. Both were signs of adoption into God's covenant, his people and his household. Jesus had invited and blessed little children so they should not be excluded. The Kingdom of Heaven belongs to them so the sign should not be denied them.

Through the Eucharist, Calvin tried to reconcile the concerns of Luther and Zwingli for the next generation. He begins by referring to God as a good father who provides a spiritual banquet for his children. The food is the Lord Jesus who gave himself up on the Cross for which his people give thanks. The signs are:

> . . . bread and wine, which represent for us the invisible food that we receive from the flesh and blood of Christ .
> . . Now Christ is the only food of our soul, and therefore our Heavenly Father invites us to Christ, that, refreshed by partaking of him, we may repeatedly gather strength until we shall have reached heavenly immortality.
>
> (*Institutes*, Bk IV.17.1)

And how is Christ present? Calvin says of the bread and the wine 'we must certainly consider them as if Christ here present were himself set before our eyes' because his words, 'This is my body . . . this is my blood' cannot lie or deceive. The words 'given for you' and 'shed for you' express the 'force' of the sacrament, for the body and blood which were once for all given up for our salvation are represented here for us [Bk IV.17.3]. The key question for Calvin is how did people receive and possess Christ? His answer was that the Holy Spirit brought Christ and his blessings to them and this was the same as saying that Christ gave himself to them. The Eucharist then confirmed the promise of Christ's words and pointed them to the Cross where that promise was enacted.

In this way Calvin took a middle way. The bread and the wine were not 'mere signs' as Zwingli was understood to claim. What was signified was present too. Eating was not just 'believing', as Zwingli had claimed, but eating followed from believing and, difficult though it was to understand, believers truly partook of Christ and so of his life through the Spirit. But Calvin accepted Zwingli's interpretation of the crucial words, 'This is my body', for Christ's body is in Heaven.

What is impressive in all these writers is that Jesus was not for them just a figure of the past but very much a figure of the present. He might be located in Heaven, or as Luther thought, everywhere, but he was their contemporary.

The Anabaptists

Christian communities sprang up under leaders who thought that Luther and his colleagues had not taken their reforming agenda far enough. These were people who called themselves brethren, or simply Christians. They were called Anabaptists, that is, re-baptizers, by their opponents. This name came from the fact that they believed and practised adult, believers, baptism. Since they had all been baptized as infants this amounted to a second baptism but they themselves did not recognize the validity of infant baptism because infants could not exercise personal faith or exhibit a change of life.

There were four main areas where Anabaptists flourished: Switzerland, Holland, south Germany and Moravia. The most noted leaders were Conrad Grebel [1498–1526] in Switzerland, Melchior Hofmann [1498–1543] in Holland, Pilgrim Marpeck [1495–1556] in south Germany and Balthasar Hubmaier [1485–1528] in Moravia. These radical reformers took the New Testament and especially the Gospels as the authoritative source of their faith and practice. But they did not always agree on their interpretations and one of the major differences was over Jesus himself.

Disagreements about Jesus

Most of them were orthodox in believing that Jesus Christ was fully human and fully divine, the only begotten Son of God, but they stressed that acknowledging this was only of any value for those who followed the example of Christ and obeyed his teaching in the way they lived. Christ had to overcome the Devil in them and through divine rebirth the Spirit of Christ within them produced real disciples living Christ-like lives.

But Hofmann and Menno Simons [1496–1561], a former Dutch priest who became the outstanding leader of the Anabaptists, had a problem with the idea that Jesus had taken his human nature from Mary. They argued that if this had been the case his humanity would have been tainted with sin and his death would have been just another human death; there would have been nothing special about it which could deal with the sins of the world. What was required was a perfect sacrifice, so they argued that Jesus brought perfect flesh from Heaven, spiritual flesh. Hofmann said that Christ passed through Mary 'as water through a pipe'. Simons put it more elegantly, comparing it to a ray of sunshine passing through a glass. The Catholics had solved this problem with the doctrine of the Immaculate Conception of the Virgin Mary. Calvin and his followers claimed the Holy Spirit had cleansed the corrupt nature of Adam in the case of Christ. Neither of these solutions convinced Simons. He claimed 'the entire Christ Jesus, both God and man, man and God, has his origin in Heaven.' But he then argued for both Christ's natural human birth as well as his supernatural origin. In this way he believed he safeguarded both the sinlessness of Christ, the reality of his humanity and his one, not twofold nature. For many this suggested the heresies of Docetism, that Jesus only appeared to be a human being, and the Monophysites, those who denied that Christ had two natures. A conference at Strasbourg in 1555 attempted to bring different sides together by acknowledging human ignorance and resolving to stick to the texts of scripture, but this was only partly successful. It is interesting that this teaching was not retained by the Mennonites, who became perfectly orthodox in their teaching about the incarnation of Christ.

The Sacraments

On the Sacraments Anabaptists dismissed infant baptism as no more than giving the baby a bath and they followed Zwingli's understanding of the Eucharist, that it was a memorial of the Crucifixion of Christ. They took the Body of Christ to be the visible congregation of the Church offering themselves in response to what Christ had done. Pilgrim Marpeck did not agree with those who claimed that the Church was a pure congregation. Rather, he said, it was where the weak and broken receive the medicine of the Great Physician, that is, Jesus himself. The rituals were physical ways in which the congregation receive grace.

Thomas Cranmer

The reformation of the Church in England involved politics. Henry VIII's problems over getting an heir were resolved by breaking the Church in England's ties with the Bishop of Rome and making the king the supreme head of the Church. But the Church authorities in England should not be dismissed as cynical politicians. Archbishop Thomas Cranmer [1489–1556] was perhaps the chief architect of the Anglican Church although its final form was established only in the reign of Queen Elizabeth, after his death. Cranmer wanted the Church in England to conform to the moderate reforms advocated on the continent and he secured the placing of the Bible in English in every parish church. Because many of the clergy were too ill-educated to write their own sermons, Cranmer had a book of sermons, or homilies, published in 1547 to which he himself contributed. Sampling one of Cranmer's sermons gives us insight into the way in which ordinary people heard about Jesus. He begins his sermon 'Of the salvation of mankind' as follows:

> Because all men be sinners and offenders against God, and breakers of his law and commandments, therefore can no man by his own acts, works or deeds (seem they never so good) be justified and made righteous before God: but every man of necessity is constrained to seek for another

righteousness or justification, to be received at God's own hands, that is to say, the remission, pardon, and forgiveness of his sins and trespasses in such things as he has offended. And this justification or righteousness, which we so receive by God's mercy and Christ's merits, embraced by faith, is taken, accepted, and allowed of God, for our perfect and full justification. For the more full understanding hereof, it is our parts and duty ever to remember the great mercy of God, how that (all the world being wrapped in sin by breaking the law) God sent his only son our saviour Christ into this world, to fulfil the law for us, and by shedding his most precious blood to make sacrifice and satisfaction, or (as it may be called) amends to his Father for our sins, to assuage his wrath and indignation conceived against us for the same.

(Seymour-Smith, p. 22)

This mirrors the teaching of Luther about justification by faith, something which human beings cannot do for themselves but can only accept from God by faith or trust alone. It summarizes the gospel of Jesus Christ, God's son, who came into the world and was obedient to the law for us, who died for us to put our relationship with God right. Cranmer goes on to say that infants are included by being baptized and people who sin again after baptism, if they repent and turn to God again, revert to their baptized state. 'Christ is now the righteousness of them that truly do believe in him.' This faith must then be expressed in good works.

Cranmer was largely responsible for the Book of Common Prayer and the Thirty-Nine Articles of 1563 were based on his

Forty-Two Articles of 1553. All ordained Anglican ministers still accept these as the basis of their faith and teaching. The first of the Thirty-Nine Articles is about the Trinity, the unity of God in three Persons. The second is about the Son, also said to be the Word of the Father, sharing the essence, or being of God, but also in one Person being truly human 'very God and very Man; who truly suffered, was crucified, dead and buried, to reconcile his Father to us and to be a sacrifice, not only for original guilt, but also for all actual sins of men'. This draws together many of the ideas about Jesus which have been debated down the centuries without attempting to explain them.

On the Eucharist ('the Lord's Supper') the Articles similarly state that it is a sign of the love Christians ought to have for each other and 'a Sacrament of our Redemption by Christ's death: insomuch that to such as rightly, worthily, and with faith, receive the same, the Bread which we break is a partaking of the Body of Christ; and likewise the Cup of Blessing is a partaking of the Blood of Christ'. The Article denies that any change takes place in the bread and the wine and says that 'the Body of Christ is given, taken, and eaten, in the Supper, only after an heavenly and spiritual manner'. It is received by faith. This was open to a variety of interpretations, something like the rhyme attributed to Elizabeth I:

> It was the Word who spake it;
> He took the bread and brake it,
> And what his word doth make it
> That I believe and take it.

The Jesuits

All the Scandinavian countries, Britain and much of Germany, Austria and France joined the reformers and cut their ties with the pope in Rome. It was not until 1545 that the Catholic authorities responded by calling the Council of Trent to carry out a programme of reform which had long seemed necessary. The Council defined Catholic doctrine on faith and grace in ways which were distinctively different from Luther, Zwingli and Calvin and defined the meaning and number of the sacraments. The Mass was defined as a true sacrifice not only of praise and thanksgiving but to eradicate the sins of the living and the dead. The real presence of Christ in the bread and the wine was affirmed with the teaching that the substance of bread and wine was changed into the body and blood of the Lord at the prayer of consecration.

But the spiritual heart of the Counter-Reformation was the Society of Jesus, established by the Spaniard Ignatius of Loyola [1495–1556], and approved by Pope Paul III in 1540. Ignatius was a former soldier whose right leg had been shattered by a cannon ball during the siege of the city of Pamplona. While he was convalescing he read a *Life of Christ* and the *Lives of the Saints*. He also had a vision of Jesus and Mary. He began to teach others about his experience of God and wrote his *Spiritual Exercises* for those who wanted to excel in their service to Jesus. His fellow students at the University of Paris founded the Society of Jesus, one of several new communities in the Church. But the Jesuits, as they became known, distinguished themselves by their dedication to education, scholarship and missionary work. Within fifty years of the death of Ignatius in 1556 there were more than 13,000 members.

As missionaries they were distinguished by their openness to indigenous cultures. In Japan, China and India they learned the languages of the people, published books in those languages and sometimes identified with them in dress and diet. Roberto de Nobili worked in Madurai in India for 49 years dressed as a Hindu monk, eating Indian food and reading the Indian sacred scriptures, the Veda, in Sanskrit. It is said he made 4,000 converts. This kind of identification with the people to whom they were sent would later be described as the incarnational principle, that is, they identified with their people just as Christ had identified with human beings.

At the same time missions tended to blend Christianity with European civilization and exploitation. This has, in recent television and popular writing, gained a bad reputation for Christian missions despite the protests of missionary priests like Las Casas [1474–1566] against the oppression and inhumanity which was sometimes involved.

Behold the Man

Proclamation in the Word and the Sacraments was a way of saying, 'Behold your God', and 'Behold the Man' as Pilate said to the crowd (John 19:5). Another way was through art and architecture. MacGregor tells the story of the building of the sanctuary at Sacro Monte in Lombardy to replicate the holy places in Jerusalem. Eventually the whole story of Jesus and its place in the cosmic plan of salvation could be traced by pilgrims moving from one chapel to another. One of the chapels has the dramatic scene where Pilate offers Jesus to the crowd with the words, 'Behold the man', as if to say, 'You decide what should be done with him'.

Pilgrims can see ordinary people and their different reactions and they are drawn into the scene as if they too have been asked to decide. This is a sermon in many dimensions.

Pictures of the Passion were also used as an aid to prayer. The viewer was reminded of Christ's great sufferings and sacrifice. Contemplating these scenes prompted remorse, repentance and thanksgiving. Albrecht Dürer [1471–1528], 'the greatest painter and engraver of the Northern Renaissance', made three printed series of scenes of the Passion with prayers in verse to accompany them. One of Christ the Man of Sorrows has the following lines:

> O cause of much great sorrow to me who is just,
>
> O bloody cause of the Cross and of my death,
>
> O man, is it not enough that I have suffered these things for you once?
>
> O cease crucifying me for new sins.
>
> (Finaldi, p. 141)

Other scenes include Jesus being flogged, crowned with thorns, presented to the crowd by Pilate, carrying the Cross and the Crucifixion. Dürer went through a deep spiritual experience and became an admirer of Luther, 'the Christian man who has helped me out of great anxieties'. Many wood engravings depicted Luther, often preaching. There is a dramatic scene by Lucas Cranach the Younger of about 1540 depicting the true church which listens to Luther and accepts the real presence of Christ in the Eucharist, represented by a lamb and the crucified Saviour on the one side, and the pope, cardinals and friars consigned to hell fires on the other.

In 1611 the Flemish painter Rubens was commissioned to paint an altarpiece for the cathedral in Antwerp. He produced a huge triptych, the central panel of which depicts the taking down of the body of Christ from the Cross. He is being lowered to the ground by means of a white linen cloth which will be used to wrap his body when it is put in the sepulchre. But this central panel stands over the altar where the body which was once sacrificed on the Cross is now made available in the Eucharist to sustain the faith of the Church which is the body of Christ in another sense. The painting captures a moment in the dynamic movement from the Cross, and the linen sheet and the body of Christ are bathed in light which also catches the faces of those lowering him. It is a striking reminder that Christ is the Light of the World. Rubens was a devout Catholic and Catholic teaching with its emphasis on the present re-offering of the sacrifice of Christ was illustrated in such a dramatic fashion.

In contrast the Calvinist Rembrandt [1606–69] who lived and worked in the newly independent Dutch Republic was not asked for altarpieces. The Protestant churches focused more on the word preached and read. Rembrandt's talents were employed on smaller paintings for teaching purposes in people's homes. He exploited both paints and engraving to capture scenes from the ministry and Crucifixion of Jesus. His paintings powerfully contrast light and darkness. In *The Adoration of the Shepherds* [1646] the infant is bathed in light and the light seems to reflect from him to those closest to him and facing us. Other figures are more in the dark and darkness looms overhead. In the foreground we see the back of one shepherd kneeling in worship, perhaps a lesson for viewers that this is the appropriate response to this child. Of other scenes Rembrandt painted perhaps the most famous is *The Return of the Prodigal Son* [1669], which has been used by more than one author to illustrate the theme of their books. The Roman Catholic Priest Henri Nouwen's meditations on this picture were widely read at the end of the 20th century. It has been said that discipleship is at the heart of Rembrandt's religious art. It is not surprising that his own experience is reflected in the different engravings of *Three Crosses*. In the first three versions light bathes Christ, the mourners and the centurion on his knees. Even the bad thief is in the light but he is blindfolded for, as MacGregor (*Seeing Salvation*) comments, salvation comes not from being in the light but being able to recognize the presence of God. The light speaks of hope, the face is calm in victory. In contrast the final two versions are darker with Christ dying in anguish for human sin. The picture almost suggests despair which may reflect Rembrandt's own sad years after his bankruptcy and the death of his wife.

Pictures in words

Towards the end of the 16th and into the 17th century, drama and poetry flourished. Robert Herrick [1591–1674] wrote a powerful poem called 'Good Friday: *Rex Tragicus*; or Christ Going to His Cross' in which the poet, taking the part of the women, addresses Christ on his way to execution and describes the crowds, the soldier with his spear, 'that sour fellow with his vinegar, his sponge and stick'. He sees the Cross as Christ's stage and his throne. Reading the poem through is like watching an action replay with commentary.

John Milton [1608–74] set the story of Jesus within the panoramic epics of *Paradise Lost* and *Paradise Regained*. As Son of God Jesus is depicted as the leader of legions of angels who drives Satan out of Heaven. He is then sent to create another world. Following the Fall he is sent to judge Adam and Eve but he prays for them. God orders their expulsion from the Garden. *Paradise Lost* concludes with news of the future incarnation of the Messiah, his death, Resurrection, ascension and second coming. Then Adam and Eve are led out of Eden. In *Paradise Regained* the Son of God reverses the sin of Adam by defeating Satan. The story begins with the baptism of Jesus by John and the acknowledgement that he is the Son of God by the heavenly voice. Then each of the temptations is vividly described and Christ rejects them. The biblical accounts in both poems are set in a wider apocryphal setting but the powerful language presents Jesus in his pre-existent roles, before he was born of Mary, as well as his incarnation.

One of the greatest Anglican poets, George Herbert [1593–1633], thus captured the message in three stanzas in contrast to Milton:

> Philosophers have measur'd mountains
> Fathom'd the depths of seas, of states, and kings,
> Walk'd with a staff to Heaven, and traced fountains:
> But there are two vast, spacious things,
> The which to measure it doth more behove
> Yet few there are, that sound them: sin, and love.
>
> Who would know sin, let him repair
> Unto Mount Olivet, there shall he see
> A Man so wrung with pains, that all his hair,

His skin, his garments bloody be.

Sin is that press and vice, which forceth pain

To hunt his cruel food through ev'ry vein.

Who knows not love, let him assay

And taste that juice, which on the Cross a pike

Did set again a-broach; then let him say,

If ever he did taste the like.

Love is that liquor sweet and most divine,

Which my God feels as blood, but I, as wine.

(Ford, p. 263)

What a powerful last line!

Chapter 7

Jesus of history
and Christ of faith

In 1892 Martin Kähler published a book with the title *The So-Called Historical Jesus and the Historic Biblical Christ*. This title contrasted the attempts to reconstruct the life of Jesus by historians with the really significant Christ of the Bible, the Christ the Apostles preached, the living Christ whom people could meet today when they respond to the preaching of the gospel. This chapter is concerned with both sides of Kähler's title, the historical search for the man who had lived in Palestine in the 1st century CE, and the faith of those who put their trust in Christ. To follow these two paths from the 18th through 20th centuries requires, instead of a chronological account, a collage which samples both themes. The chapter begins and ends with the story of the quest at each end of this historical period. In between various expressions of faith are illustrated.

Towards the end of the 17th century a significant development took place which changed the way many people in Europe, and the so-called 'Western world', thought about life, the universe, and everything. It is usually referred to as 'the Enlightenment'. It began with people trying to understand as much of the world as possible by using their reason without referring to divine revelation. They assumed that God may well have created the world in the first place but he no longer intervened in it. This belief is known as Deism. God was effectively locked out of his universe. Rationalists on the continent of Europe believed that human reason could grasp the rationality of the world. The world was thought of as a great machine so that everything could be explained in terms of the mechanical laws. It was no longer necessary to explain anything by reference to God, or supernatural agents. When Napoleon told Laplace the French astronomer that he had left God out of his calculations, he replied, 'Sire, I have no need of that hypothesis.' In Britain empiricists like John Locke [1632–1704] stressed that experience was the source of all ideas, and ideas had to be tested by experience. On this view science, or knowledge, was constructed by applying reason to empirical evidence and the assumption was that the results would be the same for everybody. All explanations could be given in terms of the observable world.

THE QUEST FOR THE HISTORICAL JESUS

This phrase comes from the title of the English translation of a book by Albert Schweitzer [1875–1965] which was published in 1910. In it he summarized many of the 19th century attempts to write a *Life of Jesus* as he really was, the Jesus of history. These writers thought that the real Jesus had been hidden beneath the Church's teaching. If they could peel off the layers of Christian interpretation they would be able to get to know Jesus as he really was. More than a touch of romanticism coloured many of these accounts. One of the most popular by Ernst Renan [1823–92] purported to recapture the experience of the first disciples walking the flower-covered hills of Galilee. Although many different 'lives of Jesus' were written in the 19th century they had certain common features. The Jesus they described was an ordinary human being. There was no room for miracles or supernatural events. After all, educated people in the 19th century knew that miracles did not happen. The important point was that Jesus had known a particularly vivid experience of God and he showed people how to live in the kingdom of God. That kingdom was already here and was growing as more people began to follow Jesus' example and to live together as children under a heavenly father. Despite his death the influence of Jesus continued to live on. This was the truth which lay behind the Resurrection stories. As stories about his teaching and deeds were passed on, occasions where he had helped people became miracles, and his close relationship with God became the teaching that he was the Son of God. Paul was chiefly to blame for turning the simple message of Jesus into the complicated theology of the Church.

As Schweitzer studied these accounts of the life of Jesus he was convinced that they all failed to describe Jesus as he really was. The biggest mistake their authors made was to assume that he was a great man like great men of the 19th century. Good men around them did not perform miracles but people could imagine them teaching the fatherhood of God and the brotherhood of man. They therefore assumed that this must have been true of Jesus and they selected material from the Gospels which demonstrated this, and rejected the rest.

Schweitzer ended his book with his own picture of Jesus, a man of the 1st century, and very much a stranger and an enigma to Schweitzer's own day. To Schweitzer Jesus was a mistaken prophet who thought the end of the world was coming before the next harvest. When that did not happen he went up to Jerusalem deliberately to force God's hand, to make him intervene in sovereign power.

> There is silence all around. The Baptist appears and cries, 'Repent for the kingdom of Heaven is at hand'. Soon after comes Jesus and in the knowledge that He is the coming Son of Man, lays hold of the wheel of the world to set it moving on that last revolution which is to bring all ordinary history to a close. It refuses to turn, and He throws Himself upon it. Then it does turn, and crushes Him. Instead of bringing in the eschatological conditions He has destroyed them. The wheel rolls onward, and the mangled body of the one immeasurably great Man, who was strong enough to think of Himself as the spiritual ruler of mankind, and to bend history to His purpose, is hanging upon it still. This is His victory and His reign. (pp. 368–69)
>
> The abiding and eternal in Jesus is absolutely independent of historical knowledge and can only be understood by contact with His spirit which is still at work in the world. In proportion as we have the Spirit of Jesus, we have the true knowledge of Jesus. (p. 401)

Schweitzer was saying that if we look for the historical Jesus in the light of our ideas of a good man we will never find him. If we take seriously the fact that he lived in a different world from ours we will find him a stranger whose career ended in failure. But his Spirit could still inspire people, like Schweitzer himself, to live lives of self-sacrifice. For all the poetic power of his writing we can be forgiven for thinking that Schweitzer himself had not attended to all that the Gospels say.

What happened to the question of Jesus and history after Schweitzer?

On the popular front the romanticism of Renan and other travellers to the Middle East informed the production of 20th century Hollywood blockbuster films such as *Ben Hur, The Greatest Story Ever Told, The Robe, King of Kings* and *Quo Vadis*. When Franco Zeffirelli's *Jesus of Nazareth* was shown on independent television in Britain in 1977 it attracted 21 million viewers. It was seen by 91 million in the USA and 84% of the Italian public were said to have seen it.

In the academic world there were three major developments. At first, in Europe in particular, interest in the historical Jesus waned. This is where Kähler's book was so influential. Others also took his line. Karl Barth [1886–1968], the Swiss theologian, stressed the great gulf between human beings and God. History, he argued, belongs to the human side of that divide. The proclaimed Christ, through whom God saves, belongs to the God-ward side. At the same time Barth insisted that the Christian message, that in Jesus Christ God became man, was an historical message. 'And only by seeing eternity and time together, God and man, only then do we grasp what is expressed by the name Jesus Christ.' For Barth Jesus Christ was the key to understanding God, the world and human beings. He accepted that Jesus was truly God and truly man although he wrote that this was a mystery. He cited John 1:14, 'The Word became flesh'. This Word, he said, was Jesus Christ and becoming a human being was his free act. He took human nature in addition to his divine nature. Then in him, God reconciled the world to himself, so that all people, not only Christians, were now reconciled to God. What was the difference between Christian believers and others? Simply that Christians knew, experienced and lived the reconciled life. This was the message Barth preached to men and women in Basel prison. He told them, 'You are free!' For Barth, faith came from hearing the good news preached, not from secular historical research. To attempt to base faith on secular history would be an attempt to give human beings a measure of control over God, instead of encouraging them to make a trusting response to the call of God. It would be an attempt at justification by works.

Another scholar whose work discouraged the quest was Rudolf Bultmann [1884–1976]. In 1921 he published *The History of the Synoptic Tradition* in which he concluded that the stories in the gospels had all been shaped, or even created, by the early Church. Consequently we could know next to nothing about the historical Jesus. Translated into contemporary terms the gospel was a call to opt for faith. Bultmann himself preached to crowded churches, often during people's lunch hour. But his account has not convinced everyone. His work on the Gospels was too sceptical about Jesus and, while he spoke eloquently of the fact that people had to make choices, he was not clear about the goal of Christian commitment.

One of the most challenging theologians of the first half of the 20th century was the German Lutheran Dietrich Bonhoeffer [1906–45]. He was executed by the Gestapo in 1945 at the age of

39. The central question of many of his writings was the question, 'Who is Jesus Christ, for us, today?' Like Luther he pointed to the theology of the Cross, the Jesus who conquers by suffering and dying. He reminded people who want to be disciples that when Jesus called people, he called them to die. This was a reference to Jesus' words about taking up a cross and following him. It was a strong way of speaking of self-denial which also, of course, might require martyrdom. He summed up Jesus as 'the man for others' and argued that in Jesus Christ God had entered the world as a human being. This set the highest value on human life so that to destroy any human being was sin. At the same time Jesus challenged our present ways of being human. He, this perfect human being, lived in utter poverty, unmarried, and died as a criminal. In these ways Bonhoeffer raised critical questions about how people are treated in society and social institutions like the state. His own life, political involvement and death demonstrated the implications of his teaching.

The quest renewed

The second development occurred in the middle of the 20th century. In 1953 Ernst Käsemann read a paper at a reunion of Bultmann's students in the presence of the great man himself. In it he argued that the early church must have had some interest in the Jesus of history to have produced the four Gospels which tell the story of Jesus' earthly life. Therefore it was likely the Gospels contained some historical information even if it was presented from the Resurrection side of Easter. Käsemann was acutely aware of the consequences of separating Jesus from his Jewish context in the light of the history of Nazi Germany. He argued that authentic sayings of Jesus could be detected by applying particular tests, the most famous of which was the criterion of dissimilarity. This worked on the basis that anything that could not have come from Judaism or from the early church, must have come from Jesus. On the basis of these criteria Käsemann highlighted the unique authority of Jesus, his association with prostitutes and tax collectors, and his saying that John the Baptist belonged to the age before the kingdom. Studies which followed these principles became known as 'The New Quest' from the title of a book by J. M. Robinson, published in 1959.

We will look at the third development in this story towards the end of this chapter but meanwhile it is clear that the concerns of the scholars did not deter ordinary Christians from sharing their faith with others.

REVIVALS OF FAITH

Alongside the growth of Enlightenment philosophies which were increasingly sceptical, remarkable renewals of faith broke out in different countries. They occurred among the Pietists in Germany, in the Awakenings in the American colonies and the Evangelical revivals in Britain. They continued into the 19th and 20th centuries with preachers such as Charles Haddon Spurgeon [1834–92], Dwight L. Moody [1837–99], and Billy Graham [b.1918]. Their impact was more than personal and found expression in the political and social work of the Clapham sect, the Salvation Army and Dr. Barnado's homes, and in the call to many to commit themselves to missionary work abroad. It would be a serious error to imagine that these revival movements were only found among the working classes. From the remarkable ministry of Charles Simeon [1782–1836] in Cambridge among the university students to Moody's addresses, these missions affected people of all classes across the social spectrum, educated and illiterate, rich and poor.

Whitefield and Wesley

The significant figures in the 18th century revival in Britain and America were George Whitefield [1714–70] and the Wesley brothers, John [1703–91] and Charles [1707–88]. These men could not help being influenced by the empiricism of their day with its stress on experience and this emphasis has continued right down to the charismatic movement of the late 20th century. Whitefield challenged people who thought they were Christians to examine their experiences. Did they have the peace of God? He then told them what they must do to enjoy God's peace. They had to be 'made to weep over' their sins and feel their need of the Redeemer. Then he quoted Jesus' words, 'Come unto me, all ye that are weary and heavy laden, and I will give you rest' and he pointed out what encouragement this offered them. He asked them if they were ever married to Jesus Christ. 'Did Jesus Christ ever give himself to you? Did you ever close with Christ by a lively faith, so as to feel Christ in your hearts so as to hear him speaking peace to your souls?' He went on at some length bringing these points home to his hearers, and all this in a sermon on a text from the Old Testament prophet Jeremiah. One can imagine the emotional challenge and the huge response from people who wanted to know the peace of God.

John Wesley preached thousands of sermons, 44 of which Methodist ministers are required to study today. It is interesting to see how few of these 44 sermons are about Christ. They are mostly about the human experience of his hearers calling them to faith and encouraging them in their Christian living. Among them are 13 sermons on Jesus' teaching in the Sermon on the Mount. The first of these includes a paragraph about the one who spoke this Sermon. 'It is the Lord of Heaven and Earth, the Creator of all; . . . the Lord our Governor . . . the great Lawgiver . . . the eternal Wisdom of the Father, . . . the God of love, who, having emptied Himself of His eternal glory, is come forth from the Father to declare His will . . . the great Prophet of the Lord.' There is an interesting fluidity here between the identity of Jesus with God and the difference between them. The assumption that Jesus was human and divine was taken for granted and never argued. Wesley was too busy bringing home to his hearers the significance of what Jesus had taught and done for them in particular. This is characteristic of many of the preachers of these revivals. They understood their role to be to expound the word of God, or 'God's Book' often verse by verse. But they took the orthodox beliefs about the Trinity and the relation of the Son to the Father for granted.

Faith in two minds

In the 19th century, increasing rationalism and secularism within the university world resulted in the publication of so-called 'assured results of biblical criticism'. For the next hundred years this threatened to undermine faith in the Bible and therefore in Jesus himself. It also provoked a parting of the ways between many of the churches and the academies although there were always scholars who served the churches and utilized their learning in defence of the faith. It is interesting to note that Spurgeon and Graham preached in much the same way as Whitefield and Wesley when allowance is made for their different social and political worlds. They were evidently addressing a need which was not met by historical studies of Jesus.

FAITH IN MUSIC

Music is a powerful means of expressing faith and bringing home the significance of Jesus to singers, players and hearers alike. In his fascinating history of Christian Music, Andrew Wilson-Dickson relates the remarkable story of Harcourt Whyte the Nigerian (pp. 285–89). Confined by leprosy to mission hospitals for 17 years he developed a deep Christian faith and wrote songs in the tonal language of the Ibo. One piece, *The Son of God was Crucified*, he wrote specially for Good Friday 1954. It was sung by the choir as they processed slowly towards their seats at the front. By the time they arrived everyone was weeping, so powerful was the effect.

Hymns

The first hymn books appeared in 17th century England. Benjamin Keach, a Baptist minister in Southwark, published a collection of his hymns in 1697. One of the outstanding of the early hymn writers was Isaac Watts [1674–1748]. His simple metres and clear summaries of Christian beliefs have given his hymns a lasting popularity. He expresses what Jesus means to each individual Christian and the impact Jesus makes on someone's life.

> When I survey the wondrous Cross
> On which the Prince of Glory died
> My richest gain I count but loss,
> And pour contempt on all my pride.

His dying Crimson like a Robe

Spreads o'er his Body on the Tree,

Then I am dead to all the Globe,

And all the Globe is dead to me.

Were the whole Realm of nature mine,

That were a Present far too small;

Love so amazing, so divine

Demands my Soul, my Life, my All.

This solemn but profound reflection of the implications of the death of Christ is expressed in wonder and with a powerful challenge; the motivation which led people to work for their Lord at home or abroad.

Probably the most widely known of the 18th century hymn writers is Charles Wesley. His hymns again express a personal response to Christ and especially to his Cross.

And can it be that I should gain

An interest in the Saviour's blood?

Died he for me, who caused his pain,

For me, who him to death pursued?

Amazing love! how can it be

That thou my God, shouldst die for me?

Jesus is clearly the Saviour who died and he is directly addressed as 'my God'. The writer and the singers are focused on something other than the niceties of the doctrine of the Trinity. That is taken for granted. It is of profound significance that people get more of their grounding in Christian beliefs through the words they sing frequently, than through the books they study or the sermons they hear.

Bach and Handel

In Lutheran countries the tradition of choral singing and organ music reached a high point with the music of Johann Sebastian Bach [1685–1750], who was hailed as 'the greatest composer that Western culture has produced'. His cantatas, written one for each Sunday of the Church's year, his *Mass in B Minor* and the great *St Matthew Passion* and *St John Passion* illustrate his stated goal of working for 'the Glory of God and the recreation of the mind'. It is music which calls for a response and the chorales express such responses. From the *St Matthew Passion*, for example, following Jesus' prediction of Peter's denial and affirmation that he is ready to die with Jesus rather than deny him, comes:

> Here would I stand beside Thee;
> Lord, bid me not depart!
> From Thee I will not sever,
> Though breaks Thy loving heart.
> When bitter pain shall hold Thee
> In agony opprest,
> Then, then will I enfold Thee
> Within my loving heart.

But, of course, you need the music, too.

Probably the most famous piece of music from the 18th century is Handel's *Messiah*. The subject is Christ himself although he remains somewhat in the background. It is in three parts. The first prepares for his coming with a judicious selection of largely Old Testament passages promising that God will act to save his people through a child. After the Pastoral Symphony the action moves to New Testament passages about the announcement of his birth. Part 2 deals with his sufferings including the moving contralto aria 'He was despised' and turns to his Resurrection and the sending out of messengers with the good news. Nations oppose the Lord but he shatters them leading to the celebration of victory in the Hallelujah Chorus. Part 3 looks forward in confidence to the Resurrection of believers and the final victory over death ending with praise to the Lamb, that is Jesus, the slain but risen Messiah.

Handel's oratorios were not far from being public entertainment, 'operas in all but name' and 18th century music in Europe in Catholic churches matched the splendour of the buildings. The Mass became a performance. By the 19th century public concerts became popular alternatives to churches as places to hear works of the best composers. There were still powerful liturgical works written by Beethoven, Berlioz, Liszt and others but they gave more attention to their secular public. Another division in the 19th century was between the music of cathedrals and parish churches on the one hand, and the popular revivalist music of the evangelists Sankey and Moody and the Salvation Army on the other. The hymns produced in this period varied from the thoughtful 'Praise to the Holiest in the height' of John Henry Newman to story-telling hymns such as Elizabeth Clephane's 'There were ninety and nine' set to a tune reminiscent of the music hall by Ira Sankey. Both were about the Gospel and about Jesus but they told the story differently.

From choirs to musicals

Until the middle years of the 20th century even nonconformist chapels had their choirs who contributed an anthem to Sunday services and on special occasions performed one of the popular oratorios. Maunder's *Olivet to Calvary* and Stainer's *Crucifixion* may not have commended themselves to everyone for their standard of music, but they were popular ways of helping many people reflect on the story of the events which led to the death of Jesus. In the second half of the 20th century these nonconformist choirs tended to disappear in Britain before the flood of what has been called 'disposable music' promoted at annual gatherings like Spring Harvest. But some of these newer songs have shown that they have staying power. Graham Kendrick's *The Servant King* is an example. Like Charles Wesley before him he identifies Christ with God without qualification but in a way that is true to Christian experience.

From Heaven you came, helpless babe,
Entered our world, Your glory veiled,
Not to be served but to serve,
And give Your life that we might live.

This is our God, the Servant King,
He calls us now to follow Him . . .

The following verses describe the sufferings of Jesus in the Garden of Gethsemane and on the Cross. Kendrick writes, 'Hands that flung stars into space, to cruel nails surrendered', and all this for the singers. It adds up to a compelling call to follow Christ's example.

So let us learn how to serve

And in our lives enthrone Him,

Each other's need to prefer,

For it is Christ we're serving.

Choral music continues in cathedrals and Anglican churches and still plays a spectacular role in nonconformist churches in North America and elsewhere. Given that Christianity is now worldwide, so is the diversity of Christian music. But the dominant theme is always Jesus. In popular entertainment, musicals like *Godspell* and *Jesus Christ Superstar* showed the continuing fascination with the person of Jesus and the events of the Gospel story. *Superstar* ran for more than 2,500 performances, becoming the longest-running musical in the history of London theatres.

TAKING THE MESSAGE OF JESUS ABROAD

The Christian faith was a missionary faith from the start and in the pages of the New Testament are stories about how Christians took the good news of Jesus to others. European missions began more than a century before the dawn of the Enlightenment. The first missions accompanied the Spanish and Portuguese adventurers on their voyages of discovery and trade in the 16th century. These missions were led by Catholic friars and especially the Jesuits. In the 17th century the Jesuit Jean de Brébeuf, working in Canada, wrote a Christmas carol for the Hurons in their own language:

Within a lodge of broken bark

The tender babe was found,

A ragged robe of rabbit skin

Enwrapp'd his beauty round;
But as the hunter braves drew nigh,
The angel song rang loud and high
Jesus your King is born, Jesus is born,
In excelsis Gloria!

(Miles, p. 354)

Apart from the Latin of the last line it reads very well in English and it shows how the familiar story was recast in terms of another culture. Catholic missionaries also had graphic visual aids in the crucifix with a man dying on a cross, and the Mass, the representation of the sacrifice of Christ. What did the Protestants have? They had a book with stories and songs.

Translating the Bible

The book was the Bible and it had to be translated into the language and culture of the people. John Eliot [1604–90] in North America learned the language of the Algonquian and translated the Bible into that language. He also preached about Jesus Christ the Saviour who could reconcile them with the great, powerful, good, Creator God, whose works were all around them. Reports of his work back in England stimulated interest which led to the formation of the Corporation for the Propagation of the Gospel in New England in 1649, the first of many missionary societies founded in the next two hundred years.

In India William Carey [1761–1834], an English Baptist, preached in different Indian languages and translated the Bible into those languages but oddly his preaching seems to have been similar in content to sermons he had preached in Northampton before he went to India. So he spoke about Jesus the Redeemer, the Saviour, 'the fountain and herald of salvation'. Even his pulpit in Serampore resembled that of an English Non-conformist Church. It took a long time before the first Hindu was converted and it cost that man, Krishna Pal, and his family, persecution from fellow Hindus. But that was the breakthrough in 1800 and by 1821 the missionaries had baptized over 1,400 new Christians.

'Conversational teaching'

In Africa converts were baptized and given British names. Some of them became agents of the mission. They took the gospel out into the market places where they engaged in 'conversational teaching'. They spoke to the immediate needs of people, needs they knew only too well. They had been taught an outline of the Bible story of salvation and related every topic to this story. That story began with the creation of the world in terms sufficiently different from African myths to arouse curiosity. It then went on to the fall of Adam and Eve. Jesus Christ was introduced as a mediator to repair the relationship between people and God. He achieved this by his one great act of self-sacrifice making all other sacrifices unnecessary. African people were used to thinking of mediators. The missionary agents then challenged them to choose between death and the life to come. In the 20th century Professor Harry Sawyer of the University of Sierra Leone argued that Jesus should be presented to Africans as the head of a Great Family which included people of different tribes and 'the idea of Jesus Christ as the first-born among many . . . can readily be introduced in this context'.

This approach which speaks of Jesus in terms familiar to the people addressed is increasingly adopted by Western missionaries.

Dr Penelope Hall has worked in Vietnam, Cambodia and Ecuador among isolated peoples. Her approach to people she meets for the first time is to listen to their stories, especially their stories about creation, the meaning of life, where they think they have come from and are going to, and what they are doing on earth. She has found that they believe in a Creator God who is good, but their immediate daily concern is to appease evil spirits. Their stories come from their ancestors and the beginning of time, or after the flood! Sometimes she has been greeted by people who knew that she had a message for them, and a message written in a book. When she told them the Bible story in outline they recognized its truth. They accepted that they deserved punishment from the Creator God for breaking his laws. But they were also expecting someone who would tell them about a Saviour. She then introduced Jesus to them in terms of their traditional religious terminology to fit the message within their mindset, the context of their story. She confirms what others have reported, that these people have 'redemptive analogies', stories, concepts and ideas in their mythologies, which can be used to tell the story of Jesus and make it meaningful to them. What is particularly interesting is how foreign this world view is to that of western sceptics, and perhaps of believers too, yet there are points of connection with biblical stories.

JESUS FOR THE WORLD

The development of theology in the 20th century has stimulated provocative ideas about Jesus in relation to all the peoples of the world. For example the Roman Catholic Karl Rahner [1904–84] combined ideas of the historical Jesus and God coming into history in him, in an evolutionary framework. Jesus Christ was the climax of God's revelation of himself. Rahner understood the world and history to be moving towards the fullness of the Kingdom of God. God himself, he claimed, was involved in this process. The Spirit of God was at work in all people, Christians and non-Christians, enabling them to become better people in the evolution towards the Kingdom. The Incarnation began this process of transforming the world. So Jesus was the focal point and goal of the development towards sharing the life of God. Human beings were free to refuse to co-operate with God but that would not prevent God's plan being fulfilled. It is not clear where the Cross fitted into Rahner's account. He also said that people did not have to recognize Jesus as God's Word explicitly. Since Christ was in all people they were all accepted implicitly. Rahner spelled his argument out in massive detail which was not always easy to follow. But like a number of other theologians, Catholic and Protestant, he seems to have been captivated by the theory of evolution as a paradigm for theology.

Other theologians trained in European universities had to revise their ways of doing theology when they went to serve people in parishes in the third world. One famous example was Gustavo Gutiérrez [b. 1928]. He told the story of how he came to Lima in Peru, and, faced with the extreme poverty of so many in his parish, asked himself how he could tell these people that Jesus Christ sets them free. What did that mean for them in the situations where they were exploited and oppressed by the rich and powerful? Like his colleagues, Gutiérrez stressed that the message of Jesus was an announcement of liberation for the poor and oppressed. Controversially the Liberation Theologians, as they are known, employed a Marxist analysis of society to determine the causes of the oppression suffered by the people. This inevitably put them in conflict with those in power, and numbers of Catholic priests lost their lives in the violence by which those governments held on to power. The theologians developed a new way of doing theology which required working alongside the poor in their struggle for a more just society. To fight against injustice was to side with Jesus. His teaching demanded that his disciples take action towards changing society. This was what living the gospel in a particular society meant.

FAITH IN ART

Whatever the intellectual questions in speaking about Jesus and the implications for living according to his teaching in the modern world, artists continued to express their faith in the ways they portrayed Jesus.

In 1848 seven artists founded the Pre-Raphaelite Brotherhood with the aim of returning to precise realism combined with powerful symbolism. So, for example, Millais' *Christ in the House of His Parents*, a picture of the young boy Jesus in the carpenter's shop, has him showing Mary a cut in his hand from which the blood has splashed his foot. To the right of the picture is a boy with a bowl of water, sometimes thought to be John the Baptist. A dove sits on a trellis above the boy Jesus. These artists tended to cram their pictures with details and every detail tells a story which needs to be decoded.

The most famous work of a Pre-Raphaelite is Holman Hunt's *The Light of the World*. Jesus is clearly recognized from the title, which comes from John 8:12. This is confirmed by the halo, the crown of thorns, the wounds and his dress which appear to combine his roles as prophet, priest and King. The light from the lantern falls on weeds growing up outside a door. He knocks on the door which has no handle on the outside and it looks as though it has not been opened in years. Hunt explained that this door was the human heart. In the Book of Revelations 3:20 Jesus says, 'Here I am! I stand at the door and knock. If anyone hears my voice and opens the door, I will come in and eat with him, and he with me'. The handle is on the inside because only the one who hears Christ can let him in. Finaldi (*Image*) contrasts this picture with Epstein's bronze figure of Christ made with a cast of the suffering face of a sick friend. Hunt's picture is the familiar Jesus but Epstein's is an unfamiliar Christ who points to his wounded hand. As Epstein explained, his Christ rebuked the world for the cruelty and suffering of the First World War.

In contrast again, Spencer's *Christ Carrying the Cross* shows him walking through the streets of Cookham, in Berkshire, where Spencer lived. This painting is bright with sunlight because the Cross brings salvation and hope. Behind Jesus are two workmen carrying ladders. These may have been necessary for the Crucifixion or are they just two men going about their work? At the same time in the foreground men carrying railings like spears recall those who went off to fight in the war. Spencer himself had served as a private soldier in the First World War and his altarpiece *The Resurrection of the Soldiers* shows how he expressed his faith in relation to that terrible carnage. The picture is littered with wooden crosses. Immediately above the altar men are emerging from the ground and being greeted by their comrades. Jesus sits in the background where he receives crosses from soldiers who bring them to him as if they are handing in their weapons. They too have laid down their lives. In the centre of the picture a young soldier stares long and hard at a crucifix (MacGregor, pp. 217–221).

If Hunt's was the most reproduced picture of the 19th century that distinction in the 20th century probably belongs to Salvador Dali's *Christ of Saint John of the Cross.* The crucified Christ is depicted somewhere above the world looking down on it with bowed head but viewers look down on him. They cannot see his face and his body has none of the familiar marks of suffering. As Dali said, 'My principal preoccupation was that my Christ would be as beautiful as the God that he is.'

But art does not always show such a high view of Jesus. In 1970 the art critic and historian H. R. Rookmaaker wrote a book called *Modern Art and the Death of a Culture* in which he claimed that modern art reflected a dying culture. One of his examples was Picasso. He wrote, 'Picasso painted more than one Crucifixion; but they were curses rather than done in faith.' Whatever one makes of that judgment, Brancusi's wooden sculpture *The Prodigal Son* is obscure to most viewers and Bacon's *Crucifixion* is almost obscene, if obsessed with guilt.

THE THIRD QUEST

From the 1970s onwards new directions in the study of the historical Jesus have been termed 'the third Quest'. One of the features of these studies has been more detailed attention to the historical setting of the ministry of Jesus in 1st century Judaism and a return to the question of his intention or purpose. Two key scholars writing in these terms are E. P. Sanders in North America and N. T. Wright in Britain.

Sanders sets out to present Jesus the human being and not Jesus the figure of Christian theology. He introduces himself as an historian and a rationalist. He recognizes that historians sometimes get things wrong and come to different conclusions but he thinks that if they work hard they can achieve modest but relatively secure results. As a rationalist he does not believe in miracles and he thinks that that is the dominant view today in contrast with the 1st century. On this basis what kind of picture does he draw?

His description of Jewish Palestine in the time of Jesus is unusual for many readers. He argues that the Jewish leaders were largely independent of Rome and the people were not oppressed by an occupying Roman army. Nor was the country on the edge of revolt although potential for war existed in Galilee and Judea. Few Jews at that time expected a Davidic Messiah and few wanted one. In this setting how does he see Jesus? He says that Jesus viewed himself as a charismatic prophet, God's last messenger and viceroy. He was an itinerant healer and teacher who travelled in the company of disciples and exercised what seemed to his opponents an arrogant authority. He began as a disciple of John the Baptist and, like John, he believed that God would soon bring a decisive change to the world, but he died a disappointed man. This is the framework for the teaching of Jesus. However great his teaching that God would create a kingdom in which Israel would know peace and gentiles would worship Israel's God, and however wonderful his ethical teaching, he was fundamentally mistaken. In Jerusalem he provoked the high priest by his attack on the temple and his talk about a kingdom, both of which marked him out as a trouble maker. The Roman governor was willing to agree to the high priest's request that Jesus should be executed. Sanders accepts that the disciples had experiences of the Resurrection appearances but he does not know what caused them.

N. T. Wright is a well-known Christian scholar, and he writes from the basis of what he calls 'critical realism' which accepts that there is factual data to deal with but the historian has to make careful judgments about them. The controlling idea in his account is that Jesus understood that God was intervening through him to bring about Israel's return from exile and through this justice and mercy would be extended to the whole world. The return which the great prophets of the Old Testament had spoken about had not taken place. Israel was still oppressed even if back in the land. Jesus saw himself as the prophet gathering Israel around himself. He issued an invitation to repent of violent revolt and believe in him as the one in whom God was acting. His healings restored people to Israel. His parables and stories were about God's intervention or Israel's response. They spoke of judgment too and on 'this generation'. The fall of Jerusalem would be that judgment and his vindication. So he attacked the temple and warned of its coming destruction. He was crucified because the Jewish leaders caught Pilate between their claim that Jesus was a revolutionary and that if he let Jesus go he was not Caesar's friend. The demonstration in the temple was a claim to be Messiah and that he was replacing the temple. The authorities saw him therefore as a false prophet. The return from exile required his death. He would defeat evil by suffering it.

Taking a different line and hitting the headlines in *Time International* in January 1994 was the work of a group of scholars calling themselves 'the Jesus Seminar'. They published a version of the Gospels called *The Five Gospels* which includes the *Gospel of Thomas* alongside the canonical four. The sayings of Jesus are colour coded according to the Seminar's view about their likely authenticity. This was established by members of the seminar voting using coloured beads. Red beads meant 'That's Jesus'; pink, 'Sure sounds like him'; grey, 'Well, maybe', and black, 'No, there's been some mistake'. On this basis only 18% of the sayings of Jesus were accepted as clearly authentic. Their portrait of Jesus is more like a wandering Greek philosopher than a Jewish prophet. One member of the Jesus Seminar, Dominic Crossan, has published his own massive biography of Jesus which represents him as a Mediterranean Jewish peasant. Other scholars have produced Jesus the sage, Jesus the visionary, Jesus the magician, Jesus the charismatic healer and so on.

What is fascinating about this is the reflection of the faith or world view of the particular scholars. There is no way of totally separating the Jesus of history from the Christ of faith and those who think that they can are misleading themselves. At the same time this does not mean there are no facts and that every writer's account of Jesus is equally valid. There is evidence about the world in which the events of the story of Jesus took place and the different portraits of different writers should drive us back to read the Gospels again for ourselves.

Chapter 8

Jesus and other religions

There is evidence to support the argument that the world is increasingly becoming 'a global village' and people are more than ever aware that different groups of people in that village have different religious beliefs and practices. While the great-grandparents of some of these people may never have heard of Jesus, for Jews and Muslims he is a significant figure in different ways and some Hindus, Buddhists and Sikhs have heard of him too. In this chapter we will consider how people of other faiths think of Jesus. What light does this throw on the essence of Jesus?

JEWISH VIEWS OF JESUS

The Jewish faith goes back to Abraham in the second millennium BCE and the belief that God chose him and his descendants for a special role in the unfolding of the divine plan to mend the world. The decisive events of Jewish history included the exodus from Egypt, the covenant between God and Israel at Mount Sinai, entry into the Promised Land, the kingdom of David, and the exile to Babylon. Although some Jews had returned from exile when

Cyrus, the conqueror of Babylon, gave all people permission to return to their own countries, the great hopes of the prophets seemed unfulfilled. This fostered hopes for a messianic king like David or a messianic age when God would put things back on course. The key Jewish beliefs were summed up by Jesus himself in two quotations from the Hebrew Scriptures, 'Hear, O Israel: The Lord our God, the Lord is one. And you shall love the Lord your God with all your heart and with all your soul and with all your mind and with all your strength.' Jesus continued, 'And you shall love your neighbour as yourself.' Of course Jesus was a Jew, talking to Jews.

Another significant aspect of the context of Jewish views of Jesus is the appalling history of persecution and suffering the Jews have endured, often at the hands of so-called Christian rulers and governments. Jews were blamed for the death of Jesus and this led to atrocities which reached a kind of climax in the Holocaust. It is not surprising that for centuries most Jews were reluctant to study Jesus or the New Testament. There was a scholar in Babylonia named Joseph Kirkisani in the 10th century who wrote that Jesus had founded a Jewish sect but that, after the Crucifixion of Jesus by the Romans, Paul had changed it into a new religion, Christianity. Some medieval Jewish commentators set out to show that Jesus had not fulfilled the Jewish Scriptures and that the time of salvation which these scriptures promised was still to come.

Claude Montefiore

Montefiore [1858–1938] was the first Jewish scholar in modern times to take a sympathetic view of Christianity. He claimed that the New Testament belonged to Jewish literature. It is true that he was selective in his treatment of the Gospels, leaving out the Gospel of John, the miracles and Jesus' messianic claims. But he admired the teaching and character of Jesus. He saw much of what was best in the Old Testament lived out in Jesus' life. He understood Jesus to be a prophet, like Amos and Isaiah, with his attack on hypocrisy and oppression and his stress on 'inwardness'. Jesus pointed to the 'higher Law of compassion and loving kindness' and he held out the hand of sympathy to the most unlikely people including women and sinners. God was his father and the father of those to whom he spoke. 'We seem to see, through the mist of eulogy and legend the sure outlines of a noble personality.' In Montefiore's view Jesus did not expect to die but thought he would live to see the new kingdom. However he was not afraid to die and was aware he was taking risks. Montefiore attributed the death of Jesus to the Sadducean priests but did not examine in detail the accounts of the trials and Crucifixion.

Joseph Klausner

Klausner [1874–1958] wrote *Jesus of Nazareth* in Hebrew. He saw Jesus as a Jewish nationalist (like Klausner himself). This accounted for Jesus' sharp response to the Canaanite woman (Matthew 15:26), his strong love for Jerusalem and his concern for 'the lost sheep of the house of Israel'. But 'there was something about him from which an"un-Jewishness" developed'. What was this 'un-Jewishness'? The all-too-extreme demands of the ethics of Jesus. The radical reduction of the Jewish Law to the law of love might be fine for the Messianic Age, but not for our world. His teaching that tax collectors and sinners were equal with good people seemed to do away with justice. His miracles were largely due to the power of 'suggestion'. He was 'obsessed by his idea that he was the Messiah' although he knew that he was different from the Messiah most people expected. The majority of his followers were the poor and ignorant who did not understand his subtle changes to the Law. The Pharisees saw it and encouraged people to turn against him. His attitude to the temple provoked the hostility of the Sadducees who had him tried and put to death. Klausner accepted the Resurrection appearances as visions. The secret of the influence of Jesus lay in the combination of strength and weakness in his personality, 'his harshness and gentleness, his clear vision combined with his cloudy visionariness – all these united to make him a force and an influence for which history has never afforded a parallel'.

Geza Vermes

Professor of Jewish studies at Oxford University and an expert on the Dead Sea Scrolls, Vermes [b. 1924–] has written a number of books about Jesus and the historical and geographical setting in which he lived. He explicitly says he is describing the Jesus of history and not the Christ of faith. Jesus was a Galilean Jew. Galilee was known for its rebellious, ignorant and uneducated people. Jesus impressed his countrymen as a charismatic teacher, healer and exorcist. His healing of the centurion's son at a distance and his authority over demons both had parallels in stories about other charismatic rabbis such as Hanina ben Dosa. 'Jesus was a Galilean Hasid (= charismatic holy man): there, as I see it, lie his greatness, and also the germ of his tragedy.' Why tragedy? He shared 'notorious Galilean chauvinism' and was unpopular with the Pharisees for his lack of expertise in the Law. On the Kingdom of Heaven Jesus believed that he and his generation belonged to its initial stages and he called on people to work for its final revelation. To enter into the Kingdom depended on letting possessions go, and unquestioning trust in and submission to God. This meant obeying the two love commandments. So why did he die? The authorities, the political establishment, saw his revolutionary teaching as contrary to the national interest. Not that Jesus himself was a revolutionary zealot although some of his followers may have been. But he was a 'victim of a preventative measure devised by the Sadducean rulers in the general interest'. He died with a cry of despair, misunderstood by friend and foe alike. On the Resurrection Vermes accepts the story of the empty tomb and rejects the idea that the disciples stole the body. But this tends to leave questions unanswered.

It is interesting how far these Jewish scholars were prepared to go and how selective they are when they deal with the New Testament. There are some disagreements in their assessment of Jesus. Was his teaching to be admired or impossible for people living in the real world? Was he unique or one of a number of similar teachers? Do they adequately account for both his death and the rise of the Christian Church?

JESUS IN ISLAM

Historically, Islam emerged in the Arabian peninsula in the 7th century CE, but theologically Muslims claim that it is the original true religion for human beings going back to Adam. They see both Jews and Christians as people who have received versions of that one true revelation but both groups had not preserved their Scriptures with sufficient care. Consequently the one true God, which is what *Allah* means, revealed his message to the prophet Muhammad between 610 and 632 CE, the year of his death. Muhammad himself was illiterate but he learned to recite the revelations which were later compiled in the *Qur'an* (which means 'recitation').

Jesus in the **Qur'an**

Christians are often surprised how much is said about Jesus in the *Qur'an*. As Ramachandra points out, Jesus is referred to in 15 different *Surahs* (chapters) in the *Qur'an* and he is mentioned 97 times in 93 verses compared with Muhammad who is mentioned only 25 times (p. 45). In *Surah* (Chapter) 19 an account of the birth of Jesus is given in words which in part recall the account of the annunciation to Mary in Luke, Chapter 1.

> And you shall recount in the Book the story of Mary . . .
> We sent to her Our Spirit in the semblance of a full-grown man . . . 'I am the messenger of your Lord,' he replied, 'and have come to give you a holy son.'
>
> 'How shall I bear a child,' she answered, 'when I am a virgin untouched by man?'
>
> 'Such is the will of your Lord,' he replied. 'That is no difficult thing for Him.'
>
> Thereupon she conceived.

A Muslim cleric preaching on this subject explained that God can create anything, simply by saying so. 'He has only to say 'Be' – and at this point the preacher flicked his fingers – and it is.' He evidently enjoyed doing this for he repeated it several times.

The account in the *Qur'an* goes on to say that Mary was criticized by her family for suspected sexual impropriety but the baby defended his mother's honour addressing them very formally from his cradle and telling them, 'I am the servant of *Allah*. He has given me the Gospel and ordained me a prophet.' This is quite an extraordinary account and attributes to Jesus a virgin birth, an honour which is not attributed to Muhammad or anyone else. Two further references relate some of the things Jesus did during his ministry. One of them tells a story which is not found in the New Testament Gospels but can be found in the *Infancy Gospel of Thomas* from the late 2nd century CE. In the *Qur'an* it reads as follows.

> When *Allah* said, O Jesus, son of Mary! Remember my favour to you and to your mother. How I strengthened you with the Holy Spirit so that you spoke from the cradle and how I taught you the Scripture and Wisdom and the Torah and the Gospel. How you shaped clay into the likeness of a bird because I let you and blew upon it and it became a bird.

The *Qur'an* goes on to speak of miracles which Jesus did by *Allah*'s permission. These include healing a man born blind and a leper, and raising the dead. Once again this goes beyond anything attributed to Muhammad. When Muhammad was asked to perform a miracle his reply was that the revelations were the only miracle for him. There is a note in the *Qur'an* which Muslims interpret as a prophecy given by Jesus that one day in the future a messenger would come, and they understand this to be a reference to Muhammad.

The two most contentious issues between Christians and Muslims are the Christian claim that Jesus was the Son of God and the claim that he died on the Cross. Many times in the *Qur'an* it is strongly denied that God fathered anyone, or that anyone should be so closely associated with God. What seems to lie behind this is the idea that Christians claim Jesus was God's son much in the way that Hercules was the son of Zeus in Greek mythology. For Muslims it is a most grievous sin 'to associate anyone with *Allah*'. It would close the gap between human beings and the Creator. Muslims also deny that Jesus died on the Cross on the basis of this revelation:

> They declared: 'We have put to death the Messiah, Jesus, the son of Mary, the Apostle of *Allah*'. They did not kill him, nor did they crucify him, but they thought they did. Those that disagreed about him were in doubt concerning his death, for what they knew about it was sheer conjecture; they were not sure that they had slain him. *Allah* lifted him up to His presence; He is mighty and wise.

Muslim judgments

A Muslim sect who call themselves the *Ahmadiya* say that Jesus was crucified but did not die on the Cross. Instead he was taken down and he revived in the cool of the tomb. Later he went to Kashmir where he eventually died. They claim to have his tombstone. Orthodox Muslims have little time for the *Ahmadiya* and they cannot accept that *Allah* would have allowed his prophet to be treated so shamefully. There are a number of references in the *Qur'an* where prophets are badly treated but then *Allah* destroys the town and rescues his servant. According to the *Qur'an* Jesus is remarkably rescued by being snatched up to Heaven. Of course the problem is that the death of Jesus on the Cross is a crucial part of the gospel for Christians.

In a recent article on the internet Michael Wolfe, a convert to Islam, summed up the Muslim view of Jesus in this way. 'Jesus' essential work was . . . to complement the legalism of the Torah with a leavening compassion rarely expressed in the older testament.' He goes on to say that Jesus was not literally the son of God in human form nor was his death an atonement for the sins of the world. Those were errors added to the Christian faith in the 4th and 5th centuries. Instead Jesus was an inspired 'teacher of wisdom with a talent for love drawn from an unbroken relationship to God'. So some Muslims revere him. Some Muslims regard Jesus as one of the world's great teachers and prophets.

Christian comment

Ramachandra regrets the fact that few Muslims read the New Testament. 'In the last two hundred years Muslims have come to rely more on the account of Jesus given in a spurious sixteenth-century document called the *Gospel of Barnabas* than they do on the *Qur'an* itself' (p. 45). He cites one glaring example. The *Qur'an* clearly teaches that Jesus is the one and only Messiah in 11 references but the *Gospel of Barnabas* makes Jesus deny that he was Messiah and assert that Muhammad was Messiah instead. On this kind of basis many Muslims assume that they know all that there is to know that matters about Jesus and this prevents them discovering more. Perhaps, as some Christians in Muslim countries have found, it is useful to draw their attention to what the *Qur'an* says about Jesus. This then raises big questions which the New Testament Gospels can help to address. There are grounds for discussion exploring the details of his message. At other points there are clear differences but patient exploration and explanation might clarify the reasons for the differences. Some degree of willingness to learn on both sides is necessary for progress in understanding.

JESUS AND HINDUISM

In some ways there is no such religion as Hinduism for the name was an outsider's word for all the people who lived across the other side of the Indus Valley in the North-West frontier region of India. That great country, India, was only united with the coming of the British and the building of the railways. But we can say that Hinduism stands for those whose world view is shaped by ancient traditional Indian ideas. They took notice of Jesus when missionaries like William Carey (see pp. 167–68) brought news of him, although according to legend the Apostle Thomas first brought the gospel to the subcontinent. There was also a kind of Hindu renaissance in the 19th century in response to British colonial power. This often took the form of reforming Indian practices and demonstrating the values of traditional Hindu beliefs.

Hindu doctrine of incarnation

Among the diverse traditions in the Indian subcontinent the one which comes closest to providing a model for Indian thinking about Jesus is devotion to Krishna. People who practise their religion in devotion to the god Vishnu are Vaishnavites and they treasure many stories of Krishna, the incarnation of the god Vishnu. One of the most widely known of these stories is found in the popular scripture the *Bhagavad Gita*. This scripture is part of one of the longest epic poems in the world, the *Mahabharata*. Krishna is disguised as the charioteer of Prince Arjuna and just before a battle they drive between the two armies and have a conversation about life and death, duty and the state of the world. Krishna explains:

> When righteousness is weak and faints, and unrighteous-
> ness exults in pride, then I come to earth. For the salva-
> tion of those who are good, for the destruction of evil in
> men, for the fulfilment of the kingdom of righteousness, I
> come to this world in the ages that pass.
>
> (*Bhagavad Gita*, 4:7–8)

This is the doctrine of *avatara* (literally 'descent') which is usually translated 'incarnation'. Krishna goes on to tell Arjuna that he has been incarnated many times before. Beliefs about the different appearances of the god Vishnu varied but eventually these stories were brought together and nine such appearances were agreed. The first three were in the form of animals who saved the world, then came a half-lion and half-man, and a dwarf. The remainder included Rama, Krishna and the Buddha. One, Kalkin, is yet to come. This teaching about god descending into living forms to rescue the world in times of crisis is superficially like the Christian doctrine of the incarnation but the differences are more important than the similarities. It is easy to see how Jesus could be incorporated into such a scheme and so misunderstood.

Mohandas 'Mahatma' Gandhi

Gandhi [1869–1948] was probably the most famous Hindu to be deeply influenced by Jesus. He had encountered Christians in

Britain and in South Africa as well as in India. He saw in Jesus'
teaching in the Sermon on the Mount the confirmation of ancient
Indian religious values of the practice of truth and non-violence.
In his book *The Message of Jesus*, Gandhi wrote:

> The message of Jesus, as I understand it, is contained in
> His Sermon on the Mount. The Spirit of the Sermon on
> the Mount competes almost on equal terms with the
> *Bhagavadgita* for the domination of my heart. It is
> the Sermon which has endeared Jesus to me.
>
> Though I cannot claim to be a Christian in the sectarian
> sense, the example of Jesus' suffering is a factor in the
> composition of my underlying faith in non-violence, which
> rules all my actions, worldly and temporal. Jesus lived and
> died in vain, if he did not teach us to regulate the whole
> of life by the eternal Law of Love.

He understood Jesus to be a revelation of the Truth which is God,
but Jesus, for Gandhi, was only one of many such revelations. He
was not unique and Gandhi valued his teaching quite independ-
ently of any concern with who Jesus actually was.

> I may say that I have never been interested in a histor-
> ical Jesus. I should not care if it were proved by someone
> that the man called Jesus never lived, and that what was
> narrated in the Gospels was a figment of the writer's
> imagination. For the Sermon on the Mount would still be
> true to me.

Keshub Chunder Sen

Of the 19th century reformers with a passionate emotional devotion to Jesus, the most enthusiastic was Keshub Chunder Sen [1838–84]. He argued that Jesus was an Asiatic and so were his first disciples. They should not then be seen in European clothing. 'Christianity was founded and developed by Asiatics and in Asia. When I recollect this my love for Jesus becomes hundredfold intensified: I feel him nearer to my heart and deeper in my national sympathies.' On this last point he wrote, 'None but Jesus ever deserved this bright, this precious diadem, India; and Jesus shall have it.' Sen spoke of Jesus in typically extravagant terms of Hindu devotion. 'My Christ, my sweet Christ, the brightest Jewel of my heart, the Necklace of my soul! For twenty years I have cherished him in my miserable heart.' He was particularly concerned to explain Christ's divinity. He referred to Christ's words 'I and the Father are one' and then explained that Christ is 'as a transparent crystal reservoir in which are the waters of divine life . . . we clearly see through Christ the God of truth and holiness'. His key concept for Christ was divine humanity and he saw Christ as a significant figure in a process of creative evolution leading to every human being becoming a human Christ by the work of the Holy Spirit. This helped him to align Hinduism and Christianity for he argued that Hindu truths and values find their fulfilment and perfection in Christ. The community he founded combined Christian and Hindu rituals and moved towards a kind of Hindu-Christian 'church'.

Pandita Ramabai

One remarkable woman, who was influenced by Sen, was Pandita Ramabai [1858–1922]. She has been called the greatest Indian woman of the past millennium. She was already travelling a similar journey. Brought up by a deeply respected father who taught her the Hindu way of devotion, she became devoted to Jesus Christ without abandoning her Hindu identity. Her relationship to God was now through Jesus and she worked tirelessly to put his radical teaching into practice by teaching and caring for widows and girls in a community called Mukti (meaning 'salvation' in many Indian languages). She criticized institutional forms of Hinduism and Christianity as distortions of faith. 'I will take Jesus as my guru. I will study the Bible for myself,' she said. She mastered Hebrew and Greek and translated the Bible into Marathi, one of the many Indian languages she spoke. She saw devotion to Jesus as a continuation of the journey she had begun with her parents.

BUDDHISTS AND JESUS

There are different kinds of Buddhists in the world and their attitudes to Jesus vary from virtually ignoring him to regarding him almost as a spiritual brother of Siddharta Gautama [561–483 BCE], the Buddha. The principal distinction among Buddhist groups is between the Theravada who claim to follow the teaching of Gautama more strictly and Mahayana Buddhists whose Buddhism developed in conjunction with other religious and philosophical ideas. This led to Mahayana Buddhism taking different forms such as Pure Land (Ching Tu) and Chan (Zen) Buddhism.

The enlightened teacher

As Gautama was a teacher, so Jesus was a teacher. As Jesus claimed to be 'the Light of the World', so Gautama was an enlightened teacher. The Buddha ('the Enlightened One') had seen how to cope with the human problem of suffering, old age and death. He saw that life was permeated with suffering, sorrow, and that everything is fundamentally unsatisfactory in our transient lives. The cause of this suffering is human craving for satisfaction in a changing world. Suffering ceases when this craving is stilled and the way to achieve this is to follow the noble eightfold path which fosters right attitudes, speech and conduct. Having made this discovery the Buddha then travelled the country in north India teaching these truths and attracting disciples. At one level, and focusing on the teaching of Jesus in the Sermon on the Mount for example, more traditional Buddhists think of Jesus as one who fulfilled a similar role for Christians.

Mahayana Buddhism

But among Mahayana Buddhists the belief developed that the Buddha was more than a human being. He was regarded as a Saviour and became the object of devotion. This development continued until he was thought of as the Supreme Reality on which all depends and was worshipped with ritual, festivals and prayer. In fact Gautama was regarded as one of many manifestations of eternal Truth, each of which was revealed in his own age. He was called *Tathegata*, meaning 'one beyond comprehension'. Clearly there is some potential here for comparison between these ideas of the Buddha and Christian ideas of Jesus. But for Buddhists, Christians spoil this possibility by claiming that Jesus is unique, the only incarnation of the divine, and his death as sacrifice to save a sinful world. Buddhists want to speak of a spirituality which goes beyond a particular person. Even the Buddha pointed not to himself but to the teaching.

A further development in Mahayana Buddhism was the *bodhisattva* idea. A *bodhisattva* is someone whose being (*sattva*) is enlightened wisdom (*bodhi*). By following the example of the Buddha these people become examples of service themselves. In Pure Land Buddhism the central figure is Amitabha, one of many who embody the *bodhisattva* ideal. But salvation is offered to any who put their trust in Amitabha. It is enough to speak his name for salvation is by grace through faith. Believers will be guided in the ship of salvation across the sea of sorrows to the western paradise. The parallels with Christian ideas are obvious in this summary but a rich mythology expresses this underlying idea in many different ways.

The Dalai Lama

The spiritual leader of Buddhists in Tibet, the Dalai Lama, is regarded as an incarnation of a heavenly *bodhisattva*, Avalokitesvara, the lord who looks down with compassion on human beings. The current Dalai Lama [b. 1935–] has lived in exile from Tibet since 1959. He has published and lectured on the teaching of Jesus. In 1994 he was guest speaker at a seminar organized by the World Community for Christian Meditation. He read passages from the Gospels and put them into Buddhist contexts. It was interesting how seldom he spoke of Jesus but in answer to a question he said that he regarded Jesus as a fully enlightened being, a *bodhisattva*. Two of the gospel passages – one on the Transfiguration of Jesus and the other on the Resurrection – gave him opportunity to explore the uniqueness of Jesus but he was preoccupied with other things.

Parallels in Zen?

Chan or Zen Buddhism was derived from a blending of Buddhist and Taoist ideas. It is anti-intellectual, experience is everything and enlightenment, *sartori*, is insight. Such insight comes not from books but can be provoked by riddles, questions and meditation. These riddles (*koans*) are impossible to answer rationally. One of the most famous is, 'What is the sound of one hand clapping?' Some have compared the use of *koans* with Jesus' use of parables, sayings such as the camel going through the eye of the needle, or even Jesus' words at the Last Supper about his body and blood. But there is no place for God as revealed in the Bible and there can be no Saviour other than ourselves.

JESUS AMONG THE SIKHS

The word 'Sikh' means 'disciple' and Sikhs think of themselves as disciples of Universal Truth. This universal truth was revealed through messengers or teachers (the meaning of 'gurus') in North India in the period 1469–1708. The first of these teachers was Guru Nanak [1469–1539], who taught that there is only one God and he is Truth. The tenth and final human teacher was Guru Gobind Singh [1666–1708], who established the Sikh brotherhood, the Khalsa, and appointed the *Guru Granth Sahib*, the revision's Scriptures, as his successor.

Sikhs draw parallels between Jesus and Guru Nanak

Both are remembered as bringing light into the world and teaching a way of life that was liberating. Each spoke as the vehicle of the Divine Voice. Their message was about inner purity and they were critical of hypocrisy. Both demonstrated the path of love towards all. The fact that martyrdom has played a significant role in Sikh history has led them to respect, if they do not understand, the death of Jesus Christ on the Cross. Dr Gopal Singh has written about the need to follow the path of the Cross.

> For to whomsoever God comes, He comes in the strangest of ways – through PAIN. Men said unto Him, 'How shall we live?' And He said, 'By dying to yourselves!' When asked, 'How shall we die?' He said, 'By being alive to what never dies within you!'
>
> (Parry, p.3)

This final comment might give rise to considerable discussion for it relies on a quotation from the teaching of Jesus that 'the Kingdom of God is within you' which may more accurately be translated 'among you'. And while it addresses the way in which everyone should live it falls well short of all that Christians understand by the Cross of Christ.

Other significant differences include the doctrine of the incarnation; that God became man in Jesus, and the exclusive claims made for Jesus. The Guru Granth quotes Guru Arjan:

> May the mouth burn by which it is said that the Lord becomes incarnate. He neither comes nor departs from this world.

Rather God appoints witnesses and works through them. They include not only the Sikh Gurus but also Jesus, Muhammad and Gandhi. So Sikhs believe that all religions lead to God; none can claim to be exclusively true or the only way of salvation.

ATHEISTS AND JESUS

Atheists, materialists, humanists, sceptics or whatever group they belong to, have a world view and a faith about life, the universe and everything including Jesus. For some of them Jesus is irrelevant, another one of those odd religious figures who matter to some people but has no significant role to play in ordinary life today. Others, like the British Humanist Association, take him more seriously. Jesus was a wandering preacher whose teaching was humanistic – surprise, surprise! Much of what he taught had been taught before, but he often put things in a fresh and memorable way. Humanists appreciate him as a teacher who added to human wisdom about how to live and make the world a better place but there is no reason to believe that he was divine, nor do we need any divine help to live well.

They believe that the New Testament writers elaborated stories about Jesus adding typically heroic features to the accounts of his life. Many of these were common in the religious ethos of the Roman world, especially in Mithraism. The problem with their account of Mithra(s), which seems to mirror many aspects of the story of Jesus, is that they go beyond the evidence. In the centuries before Christ, the god Mithra was one of many Indo-Iranian gods who changed roles over the years. Sometimes Mithra was seen as the supreme god but at other times he was guardian of kings and contracts. In the Middle East the Romans were introduced to Mithra as the bull-slayer, probably with astrological associations. The sources for the stories which humanists find parallel with the stories of Jesus come from the 3rd and 4th centuries CE, two to three hundred years after the Gospels were written. Any borrowing seems to have been the other way. It has been suggested that their motives were to demonstrate the superiority of their faith. But after the 5th century Mithraism faded away. Yet humanists suggest that the early Christians adopted these ideas from Mithraism to make their beliefs attractive to pagans. This demonstrates the value of N. T. Wright's insistence that history matters and should be done well.

As Ramachandra comments, 'the sceptic . . . still has to account for the picture the biblical narratives present of Jesus of Nazareth, and these remain the principal source of testimony concerning him' (p. 90). He goes on to ask what it was that led people to make such extraordinary truth-claims about him and to be so devoted to him within a generation after his death? These wider aspects of the historical context are important in making a satisfactory assessment.

CHRISTIANS AND PEOPLE OF OTHER FAITHS

In the second half of the 20th century, Christian philosophers like John Hick tried to modify their presentation of faith to allow for the pluralistic society. Hick argued for 'a Copernican revolution' in the way in which Christians think about other faiths. Copernicus showed that instead of the earth the sun was central to the observable world encircled by the planets including the earth. Hick said instead of seeing Christ as the centre of the universe of faiths we should see God, or Reality. Then each of the world's religions could be seen as partially true responses to Reality and each would have insights to share with others.

But as others have pointed out there are two problems with this solution. It outlaws those like Muslims or Christians who believe that their faith is the one true faith for everyone. For example,

'There is no need of the human heart which Jesus cannot meet, and that is why he belongs to east as well as west, and why no greater than Jesus will ever come – no other is required!' (Edward Norman, quoted by Milne, p. 94). It also disregards the claims of Jesus about himself and the significance of his death and Resurrection. Once again we see the need to go back to the New Testament to define how we think of Jesus.

Chapter 9

Jesus today

FIRST A WORD ABOUT 'TODAY'

For the past decade or more people have been writing about a change in 'western culture' from modernism, the legacy of the Enlightenment, to postmodernism. Some claim that this is the biggest change since the invention of the printing press or the industrial revolution. Some of the key ideas involved are the replacement of objective knowledge which is true for all, with the idea that knowledge, or truth, is constructed by human beings or communities of human beings. Consequently what is true for one person, or community, is not necessarily true for others. In one sense this is ideal for increasingly plural societies where people of different faiths live together. In such a context one would expect Hick's ideas, which we met at the end of the last chapter, to flourish. But as we saw not all people are happy with his solution and one of the stumbling blocks is Jesus Christ.

While, as we have seen, there is evidence that Jesus is respected, and even a significant figure, in some other religions, not all people of other faiths are happy to consider him. Perhaps they are afraid that their fellow believers might be attracted to him. Consequently, even in the 21st century in some countries, it is forbidden for Christians to share their faith with others, and this prohibition is enforced with the harshest penalties. This is understandable in one sense because religion, identity and culture are often bound up together. Conversion to another faith is then treason to one's own family and community. Even in former Christian countries, such as the United Kingdom, political concern to maintain harmony in a multicultural society has produced odd decisions. The replacement of Christmas and the celebration of the birth of Christ with a Winter Festival celebrating consumer demand is one thing. But in 1998, in the Lincolnshire seaside town of Mablethorpe, when Patricia Gearing's daughter died and the family marked her grave with a simple Cross, the local authority ordered that the Cross should be removed. The ruling stated that 'Crosses are discouraged as excessive use of the supreme Christian symbol is undesirable'. The family were allowed to put a headstone on the grave with a picture of Mickey Mouse on it. We obviously live in a Disney world.

At the same time, all over the world, in every country, people are turning to Jesus and acknowledging him as Lord. In the *Atlas of World Christianity* the authors give the number of 'Trinitarian Christians' for the year 2000 as over 1.7 billion, the largest religious group in the world. This atlas also shows that the centre of gravity of the Christian faith is moving southwards to Africa, Latin America and parts of Asia. In 2003 the former Beijing Bureau Chief of *Time* magazine, David Aikman, published a book entitled *Jesus in Beijing*. According to the blurb on the back cover, 'Within the next 30 years, one-third of China's population could be Christian making China one of the largest Christian nations in the world. These Christians could also be China's leaders, guiding the largest economy in the world'. For people in countries like this post-modernism is one more symptom of Western 'dis-ease' and largely irrelevant to their understanding of Jesus.

JESUS IN THE 'THIRD WORLD'

Jesus the Protector

Kwame Bediako, a distinguished Ghanaian theologian, illustrates African expressions of faith in Jesus. He quotes a translation of an illiterate Ghanaian midwife's praise of Jesus. This includes:

> If we walk with Him and we meet trouble
> we are not afraid.
> Should the devil himself become a lion
> and chase us as his prey,
> we shall have no fear
> Lamb of God!
> Satan says he is a wolf –
> Jesus stretches forth His hand,
> and look: Satan is a mouse!
> Holy One!

Bediako comments that Madam Afua Kuma's prayers and praises reflect the sense of being closely related to nature with its mysterious forces and awesome spirits. In this context Jesus Christ is known as the living 'Lord, Protector, Provider and Enabler'. Her confession of faith includes these lines:

Jesus blockades the road of death with wisdom and power.

He, the sharpest of all great swords, has made the forest
safe for hunters.

Bediako explains that this has happened since Jesus came to their part of the world. He is the 'Hero Incomparable' and with his coming the people have a 'new consciousness of God in Jesus Christ'. Jesus of the forest is Jesus of the Gospels, 'the miracleworker who does the impossible, who triumphs over the obstacles of nature, who provides food for the hungry and water for the thirsty, who delivers from all manner of ailments and who bestows the wholeness of salvation'. This Ghanaian midwife knows at first hand his presence in her work (Bediako, pp. 8–15).

Jesus the Ancestor

The South African theologian Gabriel Setiloane [d. 2004] wrote powerfully about the Cross in a context where many Africans were suffering humiliation, imprisonment and death.

And yet for us it is when He is on the Cross,
This Jesus of Nazareth, with holed hands and
open side, like a beast at a sacrifice:
When he is stripped, naked like us,
Browned and sweating water and blood in the
heat of the sun,
Yet silent,
That we cannot resist Him.

Kwesi Dickson, a leading Ghanaian theologian who quotes that affirmation of faith (in Parratt, p. 82) writes that the Cross of Jesus in an African context demonstrates both evil and triumph. Dickson sees a parallel between Paul's words, that sharing the bread and the wine in Communion is a 'participation' in the death of Christ, and African belief that death unites people in the living community. Similarly when the concept of sacrificial meals in traditional African culture is applied to the sacrifice of Christ, his death on the Cross links him and those who believe in him. Dickson adds, 'by his death he merits, to use an African image, to be looked upon as Ancestor, the greatest of ancestors, who never ceases to be one of the "living dead" because there always will be people alive who knew Him, whose lives were irreversibly affected by His life and work.' Stinton (*Jesus of Africa*) has an excellent discussion of the advantages and limitations of this portrait of Jesus. She adds others: Jesus as Life-Giver and Healer, Jesus as Loved One and Friend or member of the family, Jesus as Leader in the sense of Chief or King.

Jesus the Liberator

To move to another part of the world we can sample three essays from a collection edited by R.S. Sugirtharajah with the title, *Asian Faces of Jesus*. Rather like Latin American liberation theologians, the focus here is on the identification of Jesus with the poor and the oppressed. As the Taiwanese theologian C. S. Song writes, the real Jesus is 'the love of God that creates the miracle of life in the world. Jesus is the pain of God mingled with the pain of humanity. Jesus is the hope of God that people show in despair. Jesus is the eternal life of God which people live in the midst of death. Jesus is, lives, becomes real *when God and people reach for each other to bring about a new world out of the ruins of the old world'* (p. 146, his emphasis).

The testimony of Asian Christian women is interesting because they find Jesus liberating and empowering. Two of the essays illustrate this view. In the first Virginia Fabella says the fact that Jesus was a male is not the problem for Asian women that it is for western feminists. Theologians may sometimes make it a problem but Jesus in the Gospels lived the kind of life that is truly human and he wanted women as well as men to know this fully human life. He treated women with consideration and respect. He revealed God who cares for the weak and the poor. Asian Christian women know him as the one who has made all the difference to their lives. He is the liberator. She comments that the creeds of Nicea and Chalcedon are 'largely unintelligible to the Asian mind' (p. 217). They were for another time and culture. Today they challenge Christians to work out their own understanding of Jesus. She also suggests that calling Jesus 'Lord' in an Asian context, where lords dominate others, is unhelpful.

Chung Hyun Kyung's essay which follows also speaks of Jesus as the one who really loves and treats all people with dignity. She quotes a Christian woman from Thailand, Komol Arayapraatep:

> We women are always grateful to Jesus the Christ. It is because of him that we can see God's grace for women. God saw to it that women had a vital part in the life of Jesus the Christ from his birth to his death and Resurrection.
>
> (pp. 224–25)

Through Jesus women have come to see the life-giving aspects of their suffering and service creating the possibility of new ways of being human. In contrast to the first essay, this writer says that claiming that Jesus is Lord empowers women and frees them from the false authorities of the world. She quotes Park Soon Kyung from Korea:

> The Lordship of Christ means that his Lordship is exact opposite of patriarchal Lordship and he eschatologically places the rule of the evil powers in this world under God's judgement. Jesus put a period (an end, that is) to the power of patriarchal history by obeying to the righteousness of God as a male even to his death. His Lordship is the Lordship of the righteousness of God which is established by his suffering and death. This Lordship destroys the principality and power of the world and returns all the power and authority to God. (p. 229)

This essay examines other traditional images of Jesus and then explores some new ones such as Jesus the revolutionary, Jesus as mother, woman and shaman, Jesus as worker and grain. She draws to a conclusion with an Indian woman's poem in which she meets Jesus in the food she receives in a famine area. He comes to her in the food for the hungry people.

The editor sums up the picture of Jesus for Asian Christian women saying that they find him today 'a new lover, helper, collaborator and companion'. It is challenging to read how real the Jesus of the Gospels is in the daily lives of those who love him in such circumstances. In contrast, when we turn to the west, we find transient images of film and sensational bestsellers.

POPULAR PRESENTATIONS OF JESUS

Two headline-hitting presentations of Jesus are Mel Gibson's film, *The Passion of the Christ*, and Dan Brown's book, *The Da Vinci Code*.

The Passion of the Christ

This film whipped up a huge media frenzy and, like with many sensationalized events, the media tended to confuse issues and lose sight of what really mattered. The film deals with the last 12 hours of the life of Christ with flashbacks to his earlier ministry. This is to heighten the contrast between the compassion and care which Jesus showed towards others, and the harsh cruelty of the lashings and brutality of the Crucifixion. The film emphasizes the gory aspects and agonies of the story. After Jesus' scourging, a grief-stricken Mary goes down on her knees and mops up his blood. The impact on audiences was dramatic. Often when the film ended nobody moved and nobody spoke. Occasionally quiet sobbing was heard. It was, said one viewer, not a film to like, but an experience. Billy Graham commented, 'I doubt if there has ever been a more graphic and moving presentation of Jesus' death and Resurrection, which Christians believe are the most important events in human history. Every time I preach or speak about the Cross, the things I saw on the screen will be on my heart and mind.' It gave many opportunities for Christians to talk about Jesus to people of other faiths, including contemporary sceptics. Of course, like any other Hollywood blockbuster these days it was accompanied by sales of pendants, coffee cups, T-shirts and replica nails! It was criticized in detail on the internet by some groups of Christians who disliked Gibson's traditional Roman Catholicism and other aspects of the film but for a while it made a tremendous impact. A slightly less violent edited version has been released for those who find the realities of crucifixion too much to bear.

The Da Vinci Code

This book, published in 2003, raises a number of unusual questions. Was Jesus married to Mary Magdalene? Did they have children? Did the Catholic Church suppress these facts, and that his wife and children fled to France, because the Church wanted to protect his claim to divinity? While his book is called a novel Brown claims that it is factually true. It appears to be a kind of postmodern blurring of the distinction between fact and fiction, perhaps a kind of virtual reality. What is interesting is that much of this is not new. The novel itself acknowledges a debt to the book *Holy Blood, Holy Grail* which was published in 1982 and in 1992 Barbara Thiering wrote a book, *Jesus the Man: A New Interpretation from the Dead Sea Scrolls*, in which she claimed that Jesus had married Mary Magdalene and they had had three children, a daughter and two boys. They then divorced and Jesus married again, this time Lydia, whose story is told in the New Testament Book of Acts. All this was 'discovered' by interpreting New Testament books and other documents as written in code. It has to be said that no serious scholar has given this reconstruction any support whatever.

With *The Da Vinci Code* the secret is seen in Leonardo Da Vinci's painting of the Last Supper. On Jesus' left as we look at the painting there is a V-shape and someone who looks like a woman on the other side of the V. It is claimed that this V-shape is a symbol of a female. The woman then is identified as Mary Magdalene, an apostle among the other Apostles. Brown says that Leonardo knew the secret which the Church had long suppressed.

But what is the evidence for all this? It is not compelling. In the New Testament Gospels Mary is always mentioned in the company of other women except for her encounter with the risen Jesus in the Gospel of John Chapter 20. Here she came to the tomb and found the body of Jesus missing, a fact she reported to the other disciples. After Peter and John had investigated, Mary was approached by Jesus. She thought he was the gardener and asked where he had taken the body. Jesus spoke her name. Immediately she recognized him and grabbed hold of him. Having got him back again she did not want to let him go. This is the only encounter between the two alone. There is further evidence in two of the gnostic gospels. First, in the *Gospel of Philip* (dated in the second half of the 3rd century CE, that is, over 200 years after the time of Jesus) there is a reference to Jesus kissing Mary. The text is damaged but some scholars fill in the blanks and say Jesus kissed her on the mouth. She is also called his 'companion'. In the 2nd century *Gospel of Mary*, the other disciples talk about Jesus loving her more than them. Even if these documents are historically reliable there is still no clear evidence to support the claim that Jesus and Mary were married. The evidence for the children is even more indistinct.

It is argued that Jesus must have been married because he was a Jew and celibacy was frowned upon among the Jews. But this again is not compelling. People like the Essenes and the Qumran communities – however divided on other issues – were admired for their common commitment to celibacy. Jesus himself spoke of people who remained unmarried for the sake of the Kingdom of God. But even if he had been married that would not have counted against his divinity as the *Code* claims. It would have been another element in his humanity for which there is abundant evidence in the Gospels. Belief in his divinity came from recognizing his exceptional relationship with God, his use of divine power and authority, and the Resurrection. The claim that Jesus appointed Mary to leadership among the disciples and that this was suppressed is part of a contemporary agenda to revise orthodox Christian beliefs. Despite the support of one or two distinguished scholars, most argue that this is a distorted reading of the history of the Church.

INTRODUCING PEOPLE TO JESUS TODAY

The runaway success of books like *The Da Vinci Code* is evidence of continuing interest in Jesus in the Western world, coupled with an agenda directed towards undermining the established Church. At the same time many, in the churches, still work to create opportunities to introduce other people to Jesus as he is presented in the New Testament Gospels. Three programmes currently in use are the Alpha programme, Christianity Explored and Essence.

The Alpha course

Produced by Holy Trinity, Brompton, known as HTB, a thriving charismatic Anglican Church in London, this is currently the most widely advertised and successful means of introducing people to Jesus and the Christian faith. It has been the subject of a series of television programmes presented by David Frost. Courses are being run today in many parts of the world including Albania, Bolivia, Finland, Serbia, Namibia, Kenya, Switzerland and South Korea as well as Great Britain and North America. It is used in many different denominations including Anglican, Methodist, Baptist, Roman Catholic and the so-called 'new churches'.

So what is it? It is a series of talks on particular topics given over a period of 10 weeks supported by open discussion groups. The talks are presented either by video, tape or can be delivered live by someone at the church. They are based on a book written by Nicky Gumbel, one of the staff at HTB called *Questions of Life*. The usual format is for people to gather for a meal on a regular evening in the week. This may be followed by some singing and then the main talk followed by a break for coffee. After the break, discussion groups deal with issues raised in the talk and people are given opportunity to ask questions. Only the second and third sessions deal specifically with Jesus although he is not far away in the rest. Session 2 addresses the question, 'Who is Jesus?' and deals with the evidence for his life, death and Resurrection, each of which is treated as a matter of historical fact. Session 3 answers the question, 'Why did Jesus die?' The answer given is not in terms of the Jewish leaders, or the Roman authorities, but in terms of sin. This is understood as things people do which they know are wrong, or which they fail to do. They fail to live up to God's standards. Jesus died to pay the penalty for sin, to set free from the power of sin, to remove the pollution of sin and to remove the partition or barrier which sin creates between the individual and God. Following a testimony from someone who has accepted this before, an invitation is given to do the same. The course includes an awayday when the teaching is about the Holy Spirit. This is where the charismatic emphasis is most clearly seen because people are taught that becoming an effective Christian requires a particular experience of the Spirit.

Despite criticism from some quarters about various aspects of the programme, on the pragmatic test, does it work? The answer has to be, that in many cases it does. Many people's lives have been significantly changed and they have been drawn into a relationship with Jesus and his people in a Christian church.

Christianity Explored

To provide an alternative programme with a different emphasis, another Anglican church, All Souls' Langham Place, London, has developed Christianity Explored. Now available through conferences run all over the world, this programme is based on the Gospel of Mark. It too takes 10 weeks, and includes a weekend away. The subject of the weekend away is 'Exploring the Christian Life' and is presented before any invitation is given to commit oneself to Jesus. The weekend away includes talks about the Church, the Holy Spirit, Prayer and the Bible. The format of the evening meetings follows the same pattern as Alpha with a talk or video followed by discussion. Course members are expected to do home study on passages from the Gospel of Mark. Since the whole course is based on Mark, Jesus features more specifically in most sessions. Issues such as who he was, why he came, his death and Resurrection are explored before the weekend away. On the subject of the death of Jesus the talk begins with a quotation from Mark 10:45, 'For even the Son of Man did not come to be served, but to serve, and to give his life a ransom for many', but as far as I can see no attempt is made to explain the concept of 'ransom'. Instead attention is switched to the account of the crucifixion in Mark 15 and three points are made: God was angry, Jesus was abandoned, we can be accepted. Then the reactions of those watching Jesus die are explored. The final weeks of the course focus on Christ's call to people to become his disciples.

Essence

Both Alpha and Christianity Explored are regarded by some ministers as addressed to educated, middle-class people, although they can be adapted to other sectors of society. A programme designed for another specific target audience is Essence, developed by Rob Frost and his associates at Share Jesus International. This is deliberately designed to appeal to 'the new spiritualities people group', as Dr John Drane calls them. These are people who never go to church but whose hunger for personal spiritual renewal drives them to explore New Age types of spirituality. This programme is in six parts based on the concept of life as a journey. The 'essence' in the title is presumably the essence of Christian spirituality. One feature of the course is the revival of Ignatian contemplation, using a method devised by Ignatius of Loyola, the founder of the Jesuits. It involves taking a scene from the life of Christ and reliving it. People imagine they were actually present. They describe to themselves the details of the setting and the action perhaps through the eyes of one of the main characters, or of a bystander. It is said to be a means of entering the text in a mystical way. 'In this attitude of exploration you are in a position to attain the truth of mystery.' Later on the story of the Prodigal Son is explored using this method. In relation to the death of Christ we read, 'By receiving the love of Jesus expressed through his sacrifice made on the Cross, we discover his redeeming work in our lives and become part of the people who are reclaiming the world in his name.' Jesus plays a less prominent role in this course where the emphasis is more on meditation and the use of the senses, not just the mind. The intention is to encourage people to begin to explore Christian spirituality.

A contemporary Bible

Useful tools for introducing people to Jesus include contemporary Christian music, street theatre, dance and drama and the many new translations of the Bible which continue to pour from the presses. One of the most provocative of these recent versions is Eugene Peterson's *The Message* which is intended to present the Bible's 'tone, rhythm, events, and ideas in everyday language'. Agreed the words are sometimes more at home in a North American context (he is Professor at Regents College, Vancouver) but I'll never forget the impact they made at one Christmas carol service. In a chapel with subdued lighting and appropriately decorated, the usual carols were sung and readings read, until we came to the story of the shepherds which was taken from *The Message*. It reads like this:

> There were sheepherders camping in the neighbourhood. They had set night watches over their sheep. Suddenly, God's angel stood among them and God's glory blazed around them. They were terrified. The angel said, 'Don't be afraid. I'm here to announce a great and joyful event that is meant for everybody, worldwide: A Savior has just been born in David's town, a Savior who is Messiah and Master. This is what you're to look for: a baby wrapped in a blanket and lying in a manger'.
>
> At once the angel was joined by a huge angelic choir singing God's praises.
>
> Glory to God in the heavenly heights,
>
> Peace to all men and women on earth who please him.
>
> As the angel choir withdrew into Heaven, the

sheepherders talked it over. 'Let's get over to Bethlehem as fast as we can and see for ourselves what God has revealed to us.' They left, running, and found Mary and Joseph, and the baby lying in the manger. Seeing was believing. They told everyone they met what the angels had said about this child. All who heard the sheepherders were impressed.

Mary kept all these things to herself, holding them dear, deep within herself. The sheepherders returned and let loose, glorifying and praising God for everything they had heard and seen. It turned out exactly the way they'd been told!

The effect was electric.

THE CHALLENGE OF JESUS

What does it mean to take Jesus seriously today? In his book *Post-Christendom*, Stuart Murray argues that if Christians really followed Jesus they would be far more radically counter-cultural and subversive of the present status quo in society and the churches. He points specifically to Jesus' teaching in the Sermon on the Mount and says Jesus knew that his teaching would be more admired than obeyed. In place of comfortable and conventional religion Jesus was uncompromising in his 'approach to truth, sex, wealth, retaliation, anxiety, relationships, power, oppression, loyalty, prayer and suffering' (p. 312). Murray shows in particular how disturbing the Lord's Prayer is when the longing for the coming of God's kingdom is understood. What happens when God's will is done on earth? The hungry will be fed, debts cancelled, and forgiveness will replace revenge. In the meantime disciples battle with evil and so pray for deliverance.

Jesus not only taught but set an example in the ways he dealt with people, the stories he told, the questions he asked. He was a threat to the establishment but a friend to those on the margins of society. To follow the example of Jesus in all these ways Murray suggests would take people back to the ways Christians lived before Constantine and the political takeover of Christianity by the Roman state. He says the emphasis would be on following Jesus 'rather than only worshipping him'.

In his enthusiasm and concern to provoke radical Christian living Murray tends to overstate his point here; as if real worship could ever be an 'only'. The essence of Jesus is not that he is a radical and subversive teacher. It is more to do with who he is, and what he did, and in these respects he is unique. It is this which gives his teaching such authority. At the same time, people today live in a world which is radically different from that of 1st century Palestine, and this will affect ways in which they follow Jesus.

A more nuanced account is given by Tom Wright in his book, *The Challenge of Jesus*. In the last two chapters he outlines the significance of Jesus for the postmodern world of the west. He starts with the Cross. In some strange way, in God's plan of salvation, on the Cross, Jesus stood in for Israel and the world. Through his suffering evil was defeated, forgiveness was secured, the covenant renewed and the kingdom of God established. The disciples were commissioned to take the good news to the world and to demonstrate its reality in the ways in which they lived.

Two further striking points which Wright makes will transform the Church and the world if they are taken seriously. The first is that the bodily Resurrection of Jesus on Easter Day demonstrated that this was the first day of the new creation. The world to come came into this present world, and Jesus himself greeted his startled disciples with the greeting, 'Peace'. To elaborate on this a little, with its Hebrew background in *shalom*, peace means wholeness, well-being, security, health, prosperity and so on. It is associated with truth, reliability and faithfulness. To return to Wright, we live, he says, between the first day of the new creation and the finale. This brings us to his second powerful point. From St Paul's first letter to the Corinthians he explains that followers of Jesus are called to build on the foundation which Jesus has laid. The foundation is unrepeatable but it sets a pattern which determines the shape of the house. Disciples who build on this foundation will tell others about the salvation, healing, forgiveness, love and trust which Jesus has brought into the world and they will demonstrate the same in the ways in which they live. The power of the Holy Spirit makes this possible and it implements God's plan to reshape the world. The message of God's forgiveness for those who accept what Jesus has done carries on the obverse side a message of judgment for those who continue in their proud, self-centred greed. The underlying assumption is that all people, everywhere, are made in the image of God which means they are called to reflect God's character in their relationships with one another, their care of the created world and their worship of the One in whose image they are made. But they get it wrong, and just how wrong is exposed in our postmodern world. But the news of Jesus is the antidote for individuals, for society, and for the world.

One final point brings us to the essence of Jesus. In him, God himself was seen and heard. The one true God, the Creator of the

world, the God of Israel throughout her history of exodus, king-
doms and exile, the God of the Hebrew Scriptures; He came into
the world in Jesus and on the Cross demonstrated His love and
the extent he was prepared to go to save the world. Responding
to Jesus then is responding to God. Granted this implies a complex
view of God. But the New Testament writings bear witness to the
fact that, after his death and Resurrection, Jesus was exalted to
share the devotion and praise God's Creation before God Himself.
God is addressed in these words at the end of Revelations,
Chapter 4:

> Worthy are you, our Lord and God,
> to receive glory and honour and power,
> for you created all things,
> and by your will they existed and were created.

At the end of the following chapter in which Jesus has been
recognized as the Lamb who had been slain and by his death had
ransomed people for God we read:

> Worthy is the Lamb who was slain, to receive power and wealth
> and wisdom and might and honour and glory and blessing!

And the whole of Creation wholeheartedly sings,

> To him who sits on the throne [that is, God] and to the Lamb,
> be blessing and honour and glory and might for ever and ever!

Glossary of some religious terms

Apostle: The word comes from a Greek word meaning 'a messenger'. Jesus chose twelve of his disciples to be his special messengers. In the early Church the claim that teaching had apostolic authority meant that it went back to some of them and was therefore the standard of true Christian faith.

Annunciation: The announcement to Mary by the Archangel Gabriel that she would have a son to be called Jesus. This is closely associated with the Nativity, the story of his birth.

Charismatics: Christians who stress the use and experience of the gifts of the Spirit of God.

Church Fathers: Leaders of the Church in the period immediately following the New Testament period.

Covenant: A binding agreement between two partners in which promises are made and penalties are sometimes set out for infringements of the agreement. When the parties include God the covenant is obviously between two unequal partners.

Eucharist: The word comes from a Greek word meaning 'to give thanks'. It is one name for the Christian service also called

Holy Communion or the *Mass*, which is focused on the death of Christ.

Gentile: Someone who is not a Jew.

Gospel: Good news in the form of a message, or each of the first four books of the New Testament which tells the gospel of God at work in Jesus.

Heresy, heretical: From a word meaning 'other', this word has been used in Christian history for beliefs and practices which were different from *orthodox* beliefs and practices, that is, correct, according to the apostolic faith.

Messiah: From the Hebrew for God's special agent, a king like David, or a priest, or a prophet long-hoped-for by many Jews. The Greek word for Messiah gives us the English word *Christ*. It means the 'Anointed One'.

Passover: One of the three annual Jewish festivals. This one celebrated the great escape of the Israelites from Egypt under the leadership of Moses. It was at a Passover that Jesus was executed.

Pentecost: Another Jewish festival, fifty days after the Passover. It was on this occasion following the death of Jesus at Passover, that the disciples received the Spirit of God.

Prophet: A man or woman who speaks for God to God's people. In the Old Testament the books of prophets like Isaiah and Jeremiah contain their teaching and stories about them.

Rabbis: Jewish teachers who had disciples, those who learned from them. After the destruction of the Temple in 70 CE the Judaism which survived was led by rabbis and their teaching and known as *Rabbinic Judaism*.

Resurrection: Bodily restoration to life after death. To date only

Jesus has been raised but his Resurrection entails the promise of future resurrection for others.

Sacraments: A collective term for baptism and the Eucharist, where material objects, such as water, bread and wine, are blessed in the presence of God and take on spiritual significance.

Sin: An offence against God, either by disobeying him or failing to live according to his teaching and message.

Spirit of God: The mysterious power or presence of God and the continuing presence of Jesus Christ in the Church.

Surah: A chapter of the *Qur'an*, the holy book of Islam.

Bibliography

Atkinson, J. *The Great Light: Luther and the Reformation* (Exeter: Paternoster, 1968)

Beadle, R. & King, P. (eds) *York Mystery Plays: A Selection in Modern Spelling* [Oxford World Classics] (Oxford: OUP 1999)

Bediako, K. *Jesus in Africa: The Christian Gospel in African History and Experience* (Ghana: Regnum Africa, 2000)

Bock, D. L. *Breaking the Da Vinci Code: Answers to the Questions Everyone is Asking* (Nashville Tn: Nelson, 2004)

Chadwick, O. *A History of Christianity* (London: Weidenfeld & Nicolson, 1995)

Drury, J. *Painting the Word: Christian Pictures and Their Meanings* (London, New Haven: 1999)

Dunn, J. D. G. *Christianity in the Making, Vol. 1: Jesus Remembered* (Grand Rapids, Cambridge UK: Eerdmans, 2003)

Dyas, D. (ed) *Images of Salvation: The Story of the Bible through Medieval Art*, University of York & St John's College, 2004 [CD Rom]

Dupuis, J. *Jesus at the Encounter of World Religions* (Maryknoll,

NY: Orbis Books 1991)

Finaldi, G. *The Image of Christ: The Catalogue of the Exhibition Seeing Salvation* (London: National Gallery, 2000)

Ford, D. F. & Higton, M. (eds) *Jesus* [Oxford Readers] (Oxford: OUP, 2002)

Frend, W. H. C. *The Rise of Christianity* (London: Darton, Longman and Todd, 1984)

Frost, R. *Essence* (Eastbourne: Kingsway, 2002)

George, T. *Theology of the Reformers* (Nashville, Leicester: Broadman, Apollos, 1988)

Gumbel, N. *Questions of Life* (Eastbourne: Kingsway, 1997)

Gutiérrez, G. *A Theology of Liberation* (London: SCM, 1973)

Harries, R. *The Passion in Art* (Aldershot: Ashgate, 2004)

Jacob, W. *Christianity Through Jewish Eyes* (Cincinatti: Hebrew Union College Press, 1974)

MacGregor, N. with Langmuir, E. *Seeing Salvation: Images of Christ in Art* (New Haven & London: Yale University Press, 2000)

Manson, T. W. *The Teaching of Jesus* (Cambridge: CUP, 1955)

McManners, J. (ed) *The Oxford Illustrated History of Christianity* (Oxford: OUP 1990)

McNeil, J. T. (ed) *Calvin: Institutes of the Christian Religion*, 2 vols. (London: SCM 1961)

Miles, M. R. *The Word Made Flesh: A History of Christian Thought*, (Oxford: Blackwell, 2005)

Milne, B. *The Message of Heaven and Hell* [BST] (Leicester: IVP 2002)

Mussner, F. *Tractate on the Jews* (Philadelphia, London: Fortress, SPCK, 1984)

Murray, S. *Post-Christendom, Church and Mission in a Strange*

New World (Carlisle: Paternoster, 2004)

Nouwen, H. *The Return of the Prodigal Son: A Story of Homecoming* (London: Darton Longman and Todd, 1994)

Parker, T. H. L. *John Calvin* (Tring, Herts: Lion, 1975)

Parratt, J. (ed) *A Reader in African Christian Theology* (London: SCM, 1997)

Parry, J. 'A Possible Sikh Response to Christianity', *Joppa Group Bulletin*, Autumn 1996

Peel, J. D. Y. *Religious Encounter and the Making of the Yoruba* (Bloomington, IN: Indiana University Press, 2000)

Ramachandra, V. *Faiths in Conflict: Christian Integrity in a Multicultural World*, (Leicester: IVP, 1999)

Ryle, J. C. *Select Sermons of George Whitefield: With an Account of his Life* (Edinburgh: The Banner of Truth, 1958)

Schweitzer, A. *The Quest of the Historical Jesus* (London: Adam & Charles Black, 1954)

Seymour-Smith, M. *The English Sermon*, vol. 1 1550–1650 (Cheadle: Carcanet Press, 1976)

Snyder, C. A. *Anabaptist History and Theology* (Ontario: Pandora Press, 1997)

Stanley, B. Conversion to Christianity: The Colonisation of the Mind? *International Review of Mission*, vol. XCII.366, 2003

Stinton, D. B. *Jesus of Africa: Voices of Contemporary African Christology* (Maryknoll, NY: Orbis, 2004)

Sugirtharajah, R.S. (ed) *Asian Faces of Jesus* (London: SCM, 1993)

Thomas, N. (ed) *Classic Texts in Mission & World Christianity* (Maryknoll, NY: Orbis, 2002)

Tice, R. *Christianity Explored* (Carlisle: Authentic Lifestyle, 2003)

Vermes, G. *Jesus the Jew* (London: SCM 1983)

Wegner, P. D. *The Journey from Texts to Translations: The Origin and Development of the Bible* (Grand Rapids: Baker Books, 1999)

White, K. J. *The Art of Faith: The Story of the Bible Through the Eyes of Great Artists* (Carlisle: Hunt & Thorpe, Paternoster, 1997)

Wilson-Dickson, A. *A Brief History of Christian Music* (London: Lion, 1997)

Wolfe, M. *Islam for Today: Jesus Through a Muslim Lens*, Beliefnet.com

Wright, N. T. *The Challenge of Jesus* (London: SPCK, 2000)

Yamauchi, E. *Pre-Christian Gnosticism: A Survey of the Proposed Evidences* (London: Tyndale Press, 1973)

LOCATIONS OF SOME OF THE WORKS OF ART MENTIONED

Bacon, *Crucifixion*, Tate Britain, London

Brancusi, *The Prodigal Son*, Philadelphia Museum of Art

Dali, *Christ of Saint John of the Cross*, St Mungo Museum of Religious Life and Art, Glasgow

Epstein, *The Risen Christ*, National Galleries of Scotland

Hunt, *The Light of the World* (3 versions) St Paul's Cathedral, London; Keble College, Oxford; Manchester City Art Gallery

Millais, *Christ in the House of His Parents*, Tate Britain, London

Rembrandt, *The Adoration of the Shepherds*, Alte Pinakothek, Munich

Rembrandt, *The Return of the Prodigal Son*, The Hermitage, St Petersburg

Spencer, *Christ Carrying the Cross*, Tate Britain, London

Spencer, *The Resurrection of the Soldiers*, Sandham Memorial Chapel, Burghclere, Berkshire

Index

Abelard 120–1
Adoration of the Shepherds, The
146–7
Against the Heresies 86–7
Ahmadiya 185
Aikman, David 200–1
Akiba, Rabbi 78
Alexandria 88, 94–5
All Souls' Church, Langham
Place 211
Allah 181, 183, 184
Alpha programme 209–11
altar 132
altarpieces 106–8, 146, 172–3
Amitabha 192
Anabaptists 137–40
analogies 93
Anglican Church and
Reformation 140, 143
Annunciation, the 107
Anselm, Archbishop of
Canterbury 119–20, 134
Antioch 51
Apocalypse of Peter 85
Aquila 10
Aquinas, Thomas 121–2
Arayapraatep, Komol 204
Archelaus 22
Arians 95, 96

Arius 94–5
Arjan, Guru 194
Asian Faces of Jesus 203
Athanasius, Bishop of Alexandria
20, 95–6
Atheists 195-6
Atlas of World Christianity 200
Augustine of Hippo 93, 115,
118–19
Augustus, Emperor 25
Avalokitesvara 192
avatara 187
Awakenings 158

Bach, Johann Sebastian 113, 163
Bacon 173
Baptism of Christ, The 105
baptism
Anabaptists 137–8
Calvin's teaching 135–6
Cranmer, Thomas 141
Jesus 28–9
sacrament 128–9
bar Kokhba 77–8
Barabbas 39
Barnabas 51
Barnado's homes, Dr 158
Barth, Karl 155–6
Bediako, Kwame 201–2

Ben Hur 155
Benjamin tribe 56–7
Bernard of Clairvaux 112–13,
  114
Bethlehem 25
Bhagavad Gita 186
Bible
  contemporary 213–14
  copy in every church 140
  criticism 160
  translations 123, 126, 167–8,
    190
bibliography 221–4
Black Death 114
Blandina 90–1
bodhisattva concept 192
Bonhoeffer, Dietrich 156–7
Book of Common Prayer 141
Brahman 115
Brancusi, Constantin 173
Brébeuf, Jean de 166–7
British Humanist Association 195
Brown, Dan 206, 207–9
Bruce, F. F. 1
Buddha, The 187, 190–1
Buddhism 190–3
Bultmann, Rudolf 156, 157

Caesar, Julius 15
Caesarea Philippi 35, 42
Calvin, John 132–40
canon, definition 20
Capernaum 31
Carey, William 167–8, 186
cause and effect world 26
Celsus 81
Chalcedon formula 96, 106,
  118
Challenge of Jesus, The 215–17
Chan Buddhism 190, 193
Chester mystery cycle 110
chi-rho monogram 98, 106
Christ Carrying the Cross 172
Christ Going to His Cross 147
Christ in the House of His Parents
  171
Christ of Saint John of the Cross

173
Christianity
  1st century 74
  2nd century 11
  3rd century onwards 96–9
  4th century 99
  4th to 5th centuries 92–4
  5th to 6th centuries 101
  5th to 15th centuries 122
  7th century onwards 101–2
  16th to 17th century 147–9
  17th century 151–2
  18th to 20th centuries 151,
    158–9
  19th century 160–1
  20th century 156–8, 169–71
  1st century 199–217
  analogies used 93
  art 171–3
  boundaries 92–4
Catholic Counter-Reformation
  123
centre of gravity 200
China 200–1
classic definition of Jesus 96
Counter-Reformation 143
cross as symbol 105–7
  essential beliefs 62–3
  exploitation links 144
  hymns 161–3
  incarnation necessary for
    humanity 88–9
  Jesus as turning point in
    world history 80
  literature 147–9
  music 161–6
  musicals 165–6
  numbers in 2000 200
  official religion of Roman
    Empire 76, 92
  other faiths in general 196–7,
    199–200
  pictography 99
  pictures 171–3
  power struggles within the
    Church 101
  preaching as heart of church

worship 132
Protestant Reformation 123
sacraments, the 123, 128–31,
    139–40
separate religion 75–6
separation from Judaism 76–8,
    80–1
sermon as central feature of
    worship 123
speaks with one voice 86–7
Christianity Explored 209, 211
Christians, early
    loyalty tests 90
    persecution 89–91
    physical evidence of faith
        96–9
    Roman treatment 10–11
    vision of Jesus in victims
        90–1
Christians, first
    beliefs 62–3
    first use of name 51
    Jesus as high priest 71–2
    kingdom of God in Jesus 71
    letters 61–70
    name 51
    speeches by Paul 58–61
    speeches by Peter 54–6
    speeches recorded in the Book
        of Acts 53–4
    Stephen 53, 56
    summary of positions 73–4
    talking to outsiders 52–4
Christmas 200
Clapham sect 158
Claudius, Emperor 9–10
Clement 88
Clephane, Elizabeth 164
Codex Alexandrinus 17
Codex Sinaiticus 16–17
Codex Vaticanus 17
Commodilla catacombs 99
Constantine, Emperor 92, 94–5,
    99
conversational teaching 168–9
Copernican revolution in
    religion 196

Cornelius 55
Corporation for the Propagation
    of the Gospel in New England
    167
Corpus Christi 109
Council of Chalcedon 96, 106,
    118
Council of Constantinople 95–6
Council of Ephesus 96
Council of Jerusalem 61
Council of Nicaea 94–6
Council of Trent 143
Counter-Reformation 123
covenant 72
Cranach the Younger, Lucas
    145
Cranmer, Archbishop Thomas
    140–2
Creator God belief 169
Crick, Francis 26
criterion of dissimilarity 158
critical realism 175
cross
    African context 202–3
    central to Gospel of Mark 45
    centurion 44
    divine love 120
    film presentation 206
    Muslim views 184–5
    not allowed on gravestone
        200
    pieces of the 108–9
    stations of the 109
    symbol widely recognized
        105–7
    vision seen by Constantine 92
Crossan, Dominic 176
Crucifixion, the
    background 39
    brutal method of killing 7
    Muslim beliefs 12
    Qur'an 12
Crucifixion (music) 165
Crucifixion (painting) 173
Crusades, the 102, 109

Da Vinci Code, The 206, 207–9

Da Vinci, Leonardo 207
Dalai Lama 192
Dali, Salvador 173
dates 1
Day of Atonement 70, 72
Dead Sea Scrolls 180
Decius, Emperor 89, 91
Deism 152
Dialogue with Trypho 78–80
Diatessaron 21
Dickson, Kwesi 203
Diocletian, Emperor 91
disciples
    cannot serve two masters 36
    death before glory 35
    following Jesus 33
    self-sacrifice 35
    understanding after the event 35
disposable music 165
ditheists 77
Docetism 139
Dosa, Rabbi Hanina ben 180
Drane, John 212
Dürer, Albrecht 145

Eastern church 101–2, 117–18
Egeria 108
Eliot, John 167
Empiricism 152, 159
Enlightenment, the 151–2, 199
entering the kingdom call 32
Ephesus (Turkey) 86
Epstein, Sir Jacob 172
Erasmus 131
Essence 209, 212
essence, definition 3
Essenes 24, 208
Eucharist 105, 109, 116, 123,
    128, 130–1, 136–7, 142
Eusebius 18, 92
Evangelical revivals 158
Exiguus, Dionysius 1

Fabella, Virginia 204
faith
    framework 4
    Jesus and Christian faith not

separable 176
pluralistic society 196–7, 199
renewals 158–9
feeding of the 5,000 49
feudal system 119
films 155, 206–7
Finaldi, Gabriele 103
Five Gospels, The 176
Forty-Two Articles of 1553 142
Francesca, Piero della 105
friars 113–14
Frost, Rob 212
Frost, Sir David 209
funeral services 65

Galileans speaking in tongues 54
Galilee 22, 31
Gallic Wars 15
Gandhi, Mohandas 'Mahatma'
    187–8
Gautama, Siddharta 190–1
Gearing, Patricia 200
Gethsemane, garden of 38
Gibson, Mel 206–7
Giotto di Bondone 106
glossary 218–20
gnosticism 81, 83–9, 208
gnosticism, critics of 86–8
God
    all religions lead to 194
    gulf to human beings 155
    plan of salvation 84
    righteousness of 127–8
    sacrifice to end all sacrifices
        64–5
    whether could suffer 92–3
Godspell 166
Good Friday: *Rex Tragicus* 147
Gospels
    Apostles' connections 18–20
    contemporary accounts 21
    dates written 16
    earliest 21
    historical information 157–8
    Infancy 82, 183
    use of 21
Gospel of Barnabas 185

Gospel of John 16, 48–50, 179
Gospel of Luke 16, 46–8
Gospel of Mark 16, 19, 21, 44–6,
   211
Gospel of Mary 85, 208
Gospel of Matthew 16, 19, 21,
   40–4
Gospel of Paul 63–70
Gospel of Philip 18, 208
Gospel of the Egyptians 18
Gospel of Thomas 17–18, 83, 84,
   176
Gospel of Truth 18
Graham, Billy 158, 160–1, 206
Granth, Guru 193, 194
Greatest Story Ever Told, The 155
Grebel, Conrad 138
Gregory the Great, Pope 112
Gregory, Bishop of Nyssa 93
Grunewald, Matthias 106–7
Gumbel, Nicky 210
Gutenberg, Johann 101
Gutiérrez, Gustavo 170

Hall, Penelope 169
Handel, George Frideric 163–4
Hebrews, Book of 70–3
Heliand 111
Heloise 120–1
Heracleon 83
Herbert, George 148–9
Hermes 59, 60
Herod Antipas 22, 35
Herod Philip 22
Herod the Great 22, 23, 25
Herodotus 15
Herrick, Robert 147
Hick, John 196, 199
Hildegard, Abbess of Rupertsberg
   111
Hinduism 186–90
Hinton St Mary 99
Hippolytus 90
historical evidence 13–14
*History of the Peloponnesian
   War* 53
History of the Synoptic Tradition,

The 156
Hofmann, Melchior 138–9
Holy Blood, Holy Grail 207
Holy Trinity Church, Brompton
   (HTB) 209–11
Hubmaier, Balthasar 138
Humanists, the 195–6
Hunt, Holman 171–2
Hus, Jan 124–5
hymns 161–3

iconoclastic controversy 103–4
icons 103
Ignatius of Antioch 86
Ignatius of Loyola 143, 212
*Image of Christ: The Catalogue of the
   Exhibition Seeing Salvation* 103
*Images of Salvation: The Story
   of the Bible through Medieval Art*
   104
Imitation of Christ, The 116
Immaculate Conception of the
   Virgin Mary 139
Infancy Gospel of Thomas 82,
   183
Infancy Gospels 82, 183
Institutes of the Christian Religion
   133
Irenaeus, Bishop of Lyons 19,
   20, 21, 86–7
Iscariot, Judas 38
Isenheim monastery 106–7
Isis, cult of 25

James 9, 62
Jamnia 77
Jeremiah 37, 72
Jerusalem 22–3, 35–6, 77
Jesuits 143–4
Jesus
   arrest and trial 49–50
   Asia today 203–5
   authority unique 158
   baptism 28–9
   birth stories 41–2, 46
   born and lived in Roman
empire 22

Buddhism 190–3
circumcized 46–7
continues to be present 3
Dalai Lama 192
date of birth 1
death as 'satisfaction' 119
death, gnostics' view 85–6
divided people 32–3
documentary evidence 15–18
executed as terrorist 7, 39
Galilee 22, 31
Guru Nanak parallels 193–4
head of a Great Family 168
Hero Incomparable 202
Hinduism 186–90
historical, quest for 152–6
humanity 45, 71–2
humility 67
infancy 82
Islamic views 181–6
Jerusalem 22–3
Jewish view 177–81
Judea 22
judge 126
killed according to God's plan
    54–5
King 133–4
last journey to Jerusalem 35–6,
    41
Last Supper, the 38, 62–3
last week of life 36–7
marriage hypothesis 207–9
Messiah 47, 185
mistaken prophet 154
Muslim views 181–6
Nazareth 32–3
neither God or man 94–5
one person in two natures 96
parables 32, 36, 47
power of God 31
priest 133–4
prophet 47, 133–4
public ministry 27, 30–2
Qur'an 182–4
relation to God 92-4
relationship with individual 116
Resurrection, the 39–40, 50, 65

Saviour 47
self-denial 67
separating from Jewish
    context 157–8
Sermon on the Mount 33, 34,
    36, 160, 188, 214
Sikh beliefs 193–4
son of Abraham 41
son of David 44
Son of God 44, 183–4, 185
Son of Man 38, 43, 49
synagogues 24
Syria 22
teacher 34–5, 42, 185, 190
temple demonstrations 37
temptations 30
third world 201–5
truth embodiment 124
'un-Jewishness' 179
women 33, 204, 205
Word of God 48
world figure 169–71
Jesus Christ Superstar 166
Jesus in Beijing 200–1
*Jesus of Africa: Voices of
    Contemporary African Christology*
    203
Jesus of Nazareth (book) 179
Jesus of Nazareth (film) 155
Jesus Prayer, The 118
Jesus representations
    altarpieces 106–8
    art 171–3
    beardless youth 98
    halo 97
    icons 103–4
    medieval art 104–5
    paintings 144–7
    pictures as aids to devotion
        102–8
    shepherd 97
'Jesus Seminar, the' 175–6
*Jesus the Man: A New
    Interpretation from the Dead Sea
    Scrolls* 207
John 11
John of Damascus 104

John Rylands Library 16
John the Baptist 27–8, 29, 31,
  35, 45, 107
Joseph 25, 41–2
Josephus 8–9, 24
Judaism
  1st century 22–4
  Jewish view of Jesus 177–81
  oral law 23, 33
  protected religion 70
  rabbinic 77
  revolutionary terrorists 24
  separation of Christianity 75–8,
  80–1
  Shema 23
  three annual festivals 23, 54
  Torah 23
  traditions of the elders 23
  two ages 70–1
Judea 22
Julian of Norwich 114–16
Justin 89
Justinian 101

Kähler, Martin 151, 155
Kalkin 187
Käsemann, Ernst 157–8
Keach, Benjamin 161
Kendrick, Graham 165–6
Khalsa 193
King of Kings 155
'king of the Jews' 41
Kirkisani, Joseph 178
Klausner, Joseph 179–80
Kosiba, Simeon bar 77–8
Krishna 186–7
Kuma, Afua 201
Kyung, Chung Hyun 204
Kyung, Park Soon 205

Langmuir, Erika 103
Las Casas 144
Last Supper, The 207
Liberation Theologians 170–1
Light of the World, The 171–2
Livy 15

Locke, John 152
logos 88
Lollard preachers 124, 125
'Lord', meanings of word 67
Lord's Prayer, The 34, 35, 214
Luke 11
Lullingstone 98-9
Luther, Martin 124, 125, 126–31,
  136, 141, 145

Macgregor, Neil 103
magi 42, 43
Mahabharata 186
Mahayana Buddhism 190, 191–2
Man of Sorrows 106
Manson, T. W. 34
manuscript evidence 15–17
Marcion 19, 20, 80–1
Mark 11
Marpeck, Pilgrim 138, 140
Martha 33, 36
Martyr, Justin 19, 78–80
Mary 25, 33, 36, 106–7
Mary Magdalene 85, 107, 207–9
Mass 123, 129, 130, 143, 164
Mass in B Minor 163
Materialists 195-6
Matthew 11
Maunder, John Henry 165
Maxentius, Emperor 92
Melanchthon 128
Mennonites 139
Message of Jesus, The 188
Message, The 213–14
Messiah 163–4
Methodists 159–60
Mickey Mouse 200
Millais, Sir John Everett 171
Milton, John 147–8
Milvian Bridge, battle of 92
miracle plays 109–11
missionary work 144, 158–9,
  166–71
Mithraism 195-6
*Modern Art and the Death of a
  Culture* 173
modernism 199

Monophysites 139
monstrance 109
Montefiore, Claude 178–9
Moody, Dwight L. 158–9
Moses 49
Muhammad, Prophet 181–2, 183
Mukti community 190
Muratori, L. A. 20
Muratorian canon 20
Murray, Stuart 214–15
musicals 165–6
Muslim faith 12, 181–6
mysteries 25
mystery plays 109–11
mysticism 114–17

Nag Hammadi Library 17–18, 83
Nanak, Guru 193–4
Nativity 107
Nazareth 25, 28, 32–3, 47
Nestorius, Bishop of
    Constantinople 96
new churches 209
New Quest, The 158
new spiritualities people group 212
New Testament
    Book of Acts 53–4
    defining document 4–5
    earliest Gospel 21
    Gospels as contemporary
        accounts 21
    Gospels connections with the
        Apostles 18–20
    manuscript evidence 15–17
    selective treatment 181
    use of the Gospels 21
    see also Gospels
Newman, John Henry 164
Nicaean formula 94–6
Nobili, Roberto de 144
Nouwen, Henri 147

Octavian, Emperor 22
Olivet to Calvary 165
one hand clapping riddle 193
oral law 23, 33
Origen 88–9

Pal, Krishna 168
Palamas, Gregory, Archbishop
    of Thessalonica 117–18
Palm Sunday 109
Papias, Bishop of Hierapolis
    18–19
parables 32, 47
Paradise Lost 148
Paradise Regained 148
Passion of the Christ, The 206–7
Passover 23, 36–7
Paul
    death 89
    inclusion not implying
        exclusion of others 76–7
    letters 61–70
    persecution of Christians 56–61
    road to Damascus experience
        57–8, 63
    wisdom of God 69
Paul III, Pope 143
Pentecost 23
Peter 38, 42, 54–6, 89
Peterson, Eugene 213–14
Pharisees 23–4, 37, 57, 77
Philippian hymn 66–7
Phillips, J. B. 14
Philo 24
Picasso, Pablo 173
Pietists 158
Pilate, Pontius 22, 25, 38–9, 144
pilgrimages 108–9
Pius XI, Pope 114
Pliny the Younger 10
pluralistic society 196–7, 199
'Poor Clares' 113
Post-Christendom 214–15
postmodernism 199, 215
Pre-Raphaelite Brotherhood 171
printing 101, 125
Priscilla 10
processions 108–9
Prodigal Son, The 173
Pure Land Buddhism 190, 192

Questions of Life 210

Qumran 24, 208
Quo Vadis 155
Qur'an
    Crucifixion, the 12
    Jesus 182–4
    Jesus one and only Messiah 185

Rahner, Karl 169–70
Ramabai, Pandita 189–90
Ramachandra 185, 196
Ravenna mosaic 97
redemptive analogies 169
Reformation 123
relic veneration 108–9
Rembrandt, Hamensz van Rijn
    146–7
Renan, Ernst 152–3, 155
resurrection 50, 65, 121
Resurrection of the Soldiers, The
    172–3
Return of the Prodigal Son, The
    147
revival movements 158
revivalist music 164
road to Damascus experience
    57–8, 63
Robe, The 155
Robinson, J. M. 158
Roman Empire
    Christianity as official religion
        76, 92
    culture 25
    Greek ideas 25
    Judaism protected religion 70
    persecution of Christians 89–91
    second Jewish revolt 77–8
Rookmaaker, H. R. 173
Rubens, Peter Paul 146
Rule of St Benedict 112

sacraments, the 123, 128–31,
    139–40
Sadducees 24
St Aethelwold 104
St Benedict 112
St Clare of Assissi 113
St Domitilla catacomb 98

St Francis of Assissi 113–14
St John Passion 163
St Matthew Passion 113, 163
St Peter's, Rome 99
St Sophia's Church, Constantinople
    101
Salvation Army 158, 164
San Damiano 113
Sanders, E. P. 173–5
Sankey, Ira 164
sartori 193
Saul of Tarsus *see* Paul
Sawyer, Harry 168
sceptics 4, 195–6
Schweitzer, Albert 152–5
*Seeing Salvation: Images of
    Christ in Art* 103
Sen, Keshub Chunder 189
Sermon on the Mount 33, 34,
    36, 160, 214
Servant King, The 165–6
Setiloane, Gabriel 202
Severus, Emperor 90
shalom 216
Share Jesus International 212
Shema 23
Sikh beliefs 193–4
Simeon, Charles 158–9
Simons, Menno 138, 139
Singh, Gopal 194
Singh, Guru Gobind 193
*So-Called Historical Jesus and
    the Historic Biblical Christ, The*
    151, 155
Society of Jesus 143–4
son of David 44
Son of God was Crucified, The 161
Son of Man 43, 49
Song, C. S. 203
sources
    four Gospels 8, 82
    Jewish references 8–9
    objective accounts 12
    Roman references 9–11
Spencer, Stanley 172–3
spiritual communities 112–13
Spiritual Exercises 143

Spurgeon, Charles Haddon 158, 160–1
Stainer, Sir John 165
Staupitz 127
Stephen 53
Stinton, D. B. 203
Strasbourg conference 1555 139
Strauss, David 12–13, 26
Suetonius 9–10
Sugirtharajah, R. S. 203
Summa Theologica 121
Symeon 117–18
synagogues 24
synoptic problem 21

Tabernacles 23
table 132
Tacitus 9, 15
Taoism 193
Tathegata 191
temptations 30
Tertullian 20, 93
Theologians 117–22
Theravada 190
Thiering, Barbara 207
Third Quest, The 173–6
third world 201–5
Thirty-Nine Articles of 1563 141–2
Thomas à Kempis 116–17
Three Crosses 147
three kings 110–11
Thucydides 15, 53
Tischendorf, Constantine von 17
Torah 23, 28
traditions of the elders 23
Trajan, Emperor 10
Tree of Life 105
Trypho 78–80

'un-Jewishness' 179

Vaishnavites 186
Veda 144
Vermes, Geza 180–1
Via Dolorosa 109
Virgin Mary 107, 139

Vishnu 186–7

Watts, Isaac 161–2
Wesley, Charles 159, 162, 165
Wesley, John 159–60
Western church 101–2, 118–19
Westminster Abbey 107–8
When I survey the wondrous cross 161–2
Whitefield, George 159, 160
Whyte, Harcourt 161
'wilderness' definition 27–8
Wilson-Dickson, Andrew 161
Winter Festival 200
Wolfe, Michael 185
Word of God 48
World Community for Christian Meditation seminar 1994 192
Wright, N. T. 173, 175, 196
Wright, Tom 215-17
Wyclif, John 124

York mystery cycle 110

Zacchaeus 47
zealots 24
Zeffirelli, Franco 155
Zen Buddhism 190, 193
Zeus 59, 60, 80
Zwingli, Ulrich 129–32, 136, 137